EARLY FIREARMS 1300–1800

Michael Spencer

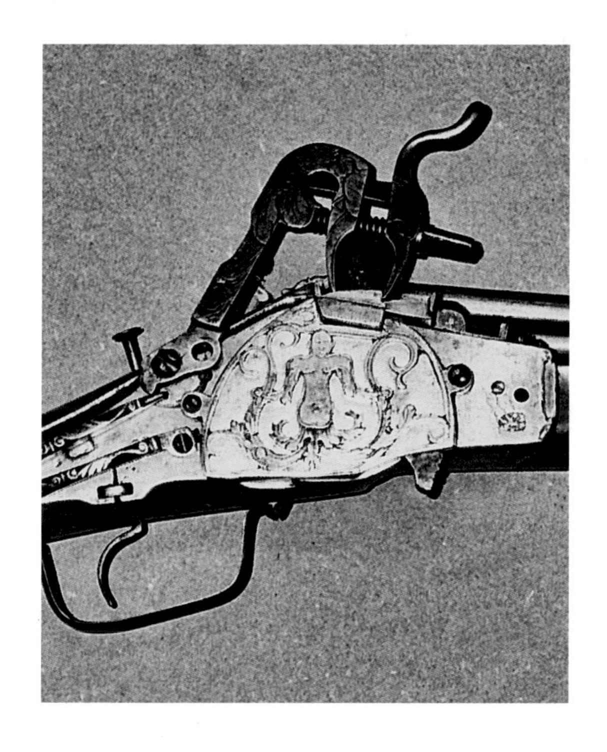

SHIRE PUBLICATIONS

First published in Great Britain in 2008 by Shire Publications Ltd,
Midland House, West Way, Botley, Oxford OX2 0PH, United Kingdom.
443 Park Avenue South, New York, NY 10016, USA.

E-mail: shire@shirebooks.co.uk • www.shirebooks.co.uk

A CIP catalog record for this book is available from the British Library.

Shire Library no. 464 • ISBN-13: 978 0 7478 0672 1

Michael Spencer has asserted his right under the Copyright, Designs and Patents Act, 1988,
to be identified as the author of this book.

Designed by Ken Vail Graphic Design, Cambridge, UK and typeset in Perpetua and Gill Sans.
Printed in Malta by Gutenberg Press Ltd.

08 09 10 11 12 10 9 8 7 6 5 4 3 2

COVER IMAGE

Detail of wheellock gun: Italian, perhaps from Sicily, *c.*1650. See picture on page 13 (centre). (Liverpool Museum, no. M.4761. © National Museums, Liverpool)

TITLE PAGE IMAGE

Three-barrelled wheellock self-spanning, so-called 'segment' lock revolver: German (Nuremberg), *c.*1570. (Kelvingrove Museum, Glasgow, no. 1939.65.yn. Photography allowed by kind permission of Glasgow Museums)

CONTENTS PAGE IMAGE

Wheellock rifle: Silesian, *c.*1645. See picture on page 12. (Pitt-Rivers Museum, Oxford, no. 1884.27.21)

ACKNOWLEDGEMENTS

The author would like to thank Marina de Alarcón and Michael O'Hanlon of the Pitt-Rivers Museum, Oxford; Tobias Capwell of the Wallace Collection, London and formerly of Kelvingrove Museum, Glasgow; Michael Gilroy of the Royal Armouries, Leeds; Amanda Turner of the Ashmolean Museum, Oxford; Winnie Tyrell of Glasgow Museums, and Sharon Wylie of the National Museums, Liverpool for their help and co-operation in preparing the illustrations for this book. He would also particularly like to thank Helen Spencer for her encouragement and advice throughout, and Oliver Spencer for taking most of the colour photographs and typing the manuscript.

Shire Publications is supporting the Woodland Trust, the UK's leading woodland conservation charity, by funding the dedication of trees.

CONTENTS

ORIGINS	4
THE ERA OF THE WHEELLOCK	12
THE DEVELOPMENT OF THE FLINTLOCK	24
THE EIGHTEENTH CENTURY	36
POSTSCRIPT	46
FURTHER READING	47
PLACES TO VISIT	47
INDEX	48

ORIGINS

Uffano reporteth, that the invention and use as well of Ordnance as of Gunne-powder was … made knowne and practized in the great and ingenious Kingdome of China, and that in the Maratyne Provinces thereof, there yet remaine certaine Peeces of Ordnance, both of Iron and Brasse, with the memory of their yeeres of Foundings ingraved upon them.

Robert Norton (1628), *The Gunner, shewing the Whole Practice of Artillery.*

THERE seems little doubt that China was the birthplace of both gunpowder and the gun. The earliest literary mention of gunpowder is in the *Wu Ching Tsung Yao* ('Collection of the Most Important Military Techniques'), completed in 1044, but there is evidence for the existence of primitive compositions as early as the ninth century. The transformation of early Roman candle-like weapons into the gun proper, using an explosion produced by a fast-burning gunpowder composed of saltpetre (potassium nitrate), sulphur and charcoal to expel a projectile (the chemical reaction is approximately: $2KNO_3 + S + 3C \rightarrow K_2S + N_2 + 3CO_2$), had been accomplished by the end of the thirteenth century, and what has been claimed as the earliest surviving such firearm – a bronze piece found in Heilungchiang province in Manchuria – appears to date from this period. The earliest known

Iron hand-gun: German(?), late fifteenth century. The recoil hook is clearly visible; the German name for this type of gun – *Hakenbüchse* ('hook-gun') – was the origin of the archaic term 'arquebus'. (Pitt-Rivers Museum, Oxford, no. 1884.27.1)

European example is probably that from Loshult in Sweden, now in the National Historical Museum in Stockholm (no. 2891), whose flask shape relates it to an arrow-firing cannon depicted in an English manuscript of 1327, *De Nobilitatibus, Sapientiis et Prudentiis Regum* ('On the Majesty, Wisdom and Prudence of Kings') by Walter de Milemete, preserved in the library of Christ Church College, Oxford (MS.92).

Although numerous firearms of Chinese manufacture (frequently dated – one as early as 1332) survive from the fourteenth century, European pieces of this antiquity are rare. All these weapons were loaded from the muzzle with powder and lead ball – rammed to the breech with a ramrod – and were fired by the application of a smouldering slow-match (cord impregnated with saltpetre) to a small touch-hole on the upper surface of the breech which communicated with the main powder charge. The touch-hole was often surrounded by a shallow depression, forming a rudimentary flash-pan, in which priming powder could be heaped to facilitate ignition. The majority of hand-guns (which at this time differed only in size from weapons which would today be described as cannon) in both East and West were provided with a socket at the breech into which a wooden tiller, or pole to facilitate

Below:
Breech end of the gun illustrated on page 4. The barrel of the gun is prolonged into a socket for the wooden tiller, now missing. The touch-hole is also visible.

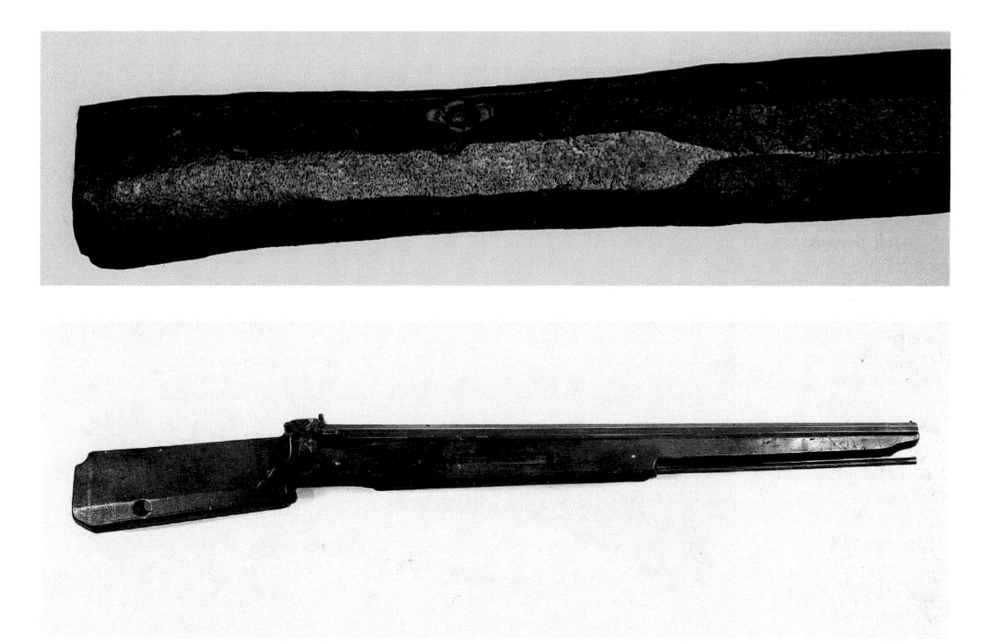

Matchlock gun: German, c.1500. The barrel is of bronze and is provided with front and rear sights. A snap-matchlock was originally fitted, its parts secured directly to the wood of the stock. The ramrod is housed in the fore-stock, below the barrel; this was to remain the standard arrangement. (Royal Armouries, Leeds, no. XII.1787. © The Board of Trustees of the Armouries)

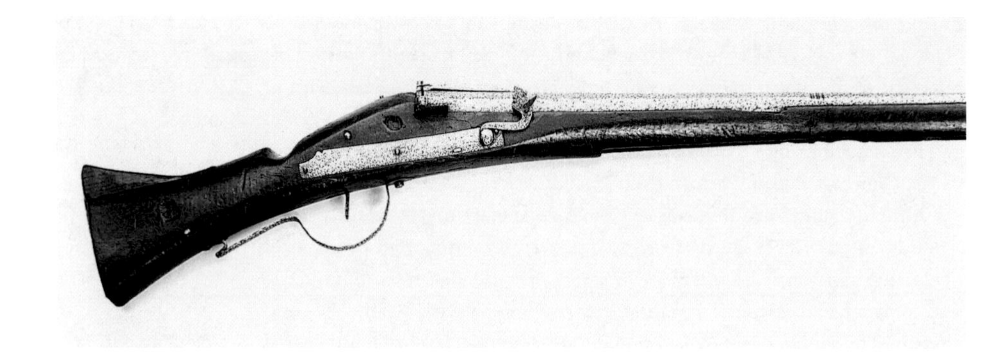

Above: Matchlock musket: English, *c.*1600. The mechanism became the commonest European type. Pressure on the trigger caused the serpentine holding the matchcord to dip into the flash-pan. Lewis de Gaya's *Art of War* of 1678 defines a musket as 'a Weapon for Foot, the barrel of which is three foot and eight inches long [112 cm], mounted on a stock of four foot and eight inches [142 cm] in length'; the calibre was usually of the order of three quarters of an inch (19 mm). Introduced around the middle of the sixteenth century, it was to remain – with a variety of lock types – the standard firearm of European infantry until the middle of the nineteenth century. (Courtesy of Wallis & Wallis)

handling, could be fastened – the ancestor of all later gun stocks. A common feature of European, but not of Chinese, constructional practice was the provision of a projecting lug on the underside of the barrel near the muzzle which could be hooked over a rampart to absorb the recoil on firing.

A primitive matchlock, in which the smouldering matchcord was dipped into the flash-pan by means of a mechanical arm, or 'serpentine', appears to have been in limited use in Europe by the early fifteenth century. The earliest known depiction of such a mechanism appears on an illustration in a German

Below: Matchlock musket: Swiss(?), *c.*1620. Although this weapon is of military design, its fine quality implies that it was intended for a wealthy owner. The lock is activated by a long sear lever, rather than a conventional trigger; this is a primitive arrangement, derived from crossbow constructional practice. (Pitt-Rivers Museum, Oxford, no. 1884.27.17)

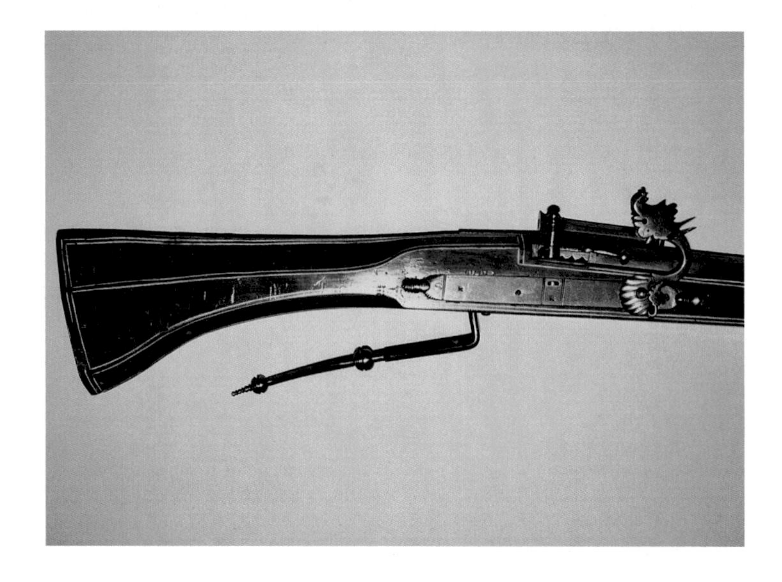

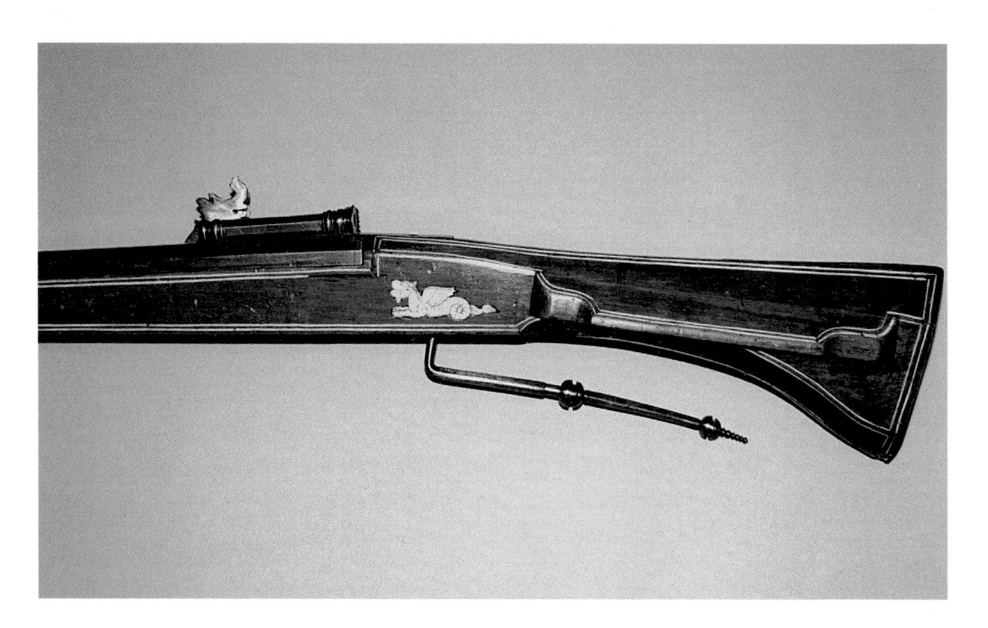

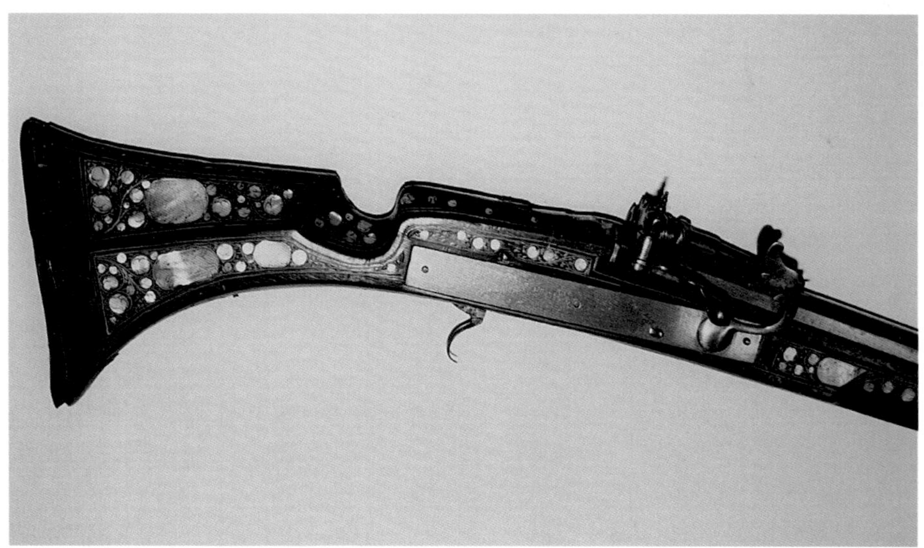

Top: Left-hand side of the musket illustrated on page 6 (bottom). The white material inlaid into the wood of the stock is bone.

Bottom: Matchlock musket: Dutch, *c.*1620. This is a decorated version of the standard military musket of the first half of the seventeenth century. The stock is inlaid with brass wire and mother-of-pearl. Very similar pieces were manufactured in England. (Liverpool Museum, no. M.4763. © National Museums, Liverpool)

manuscript of 1411 in the Austrian National Library in Vienna (Codex MS.3069). It may nonetheless have originated in China, in which case it was the last significant contribution made by that nation to the development of hand firearms.

Although the socketed type of hand-gun continued to be made in Europe until around 1500, the tendency during the fifteenth century was towards lightening the barrel, and with this the replacement of the old tiller by a more sophisticated stock which extended under the barrel to support it, and where provision was also made for housing the wooden ramrod. During the latter part of the century the matchlock mechanism increased in complexity, frequently taking the form of a spring-operated snapping mechanism situated on the right-hand side of the stock. Initially, the mechanical parts were secured directly to the wood of the stock, and were not mounted together on a detachable metal lockplate, such as later became standard practice. The flash-pan, provided with a manually operated pivoting cover, now took the form of a metal trough situated on the right-hand side of the breech; in due course it would become part of the lockplate. The barrels themselves were of either iron or bronze.

By 1500, a variety of such mechanisms was in use, of varying degrees of sophistication. The cheapness, simplicity and robustness of the matchlock ensured its popularity in European military circles until the end of the

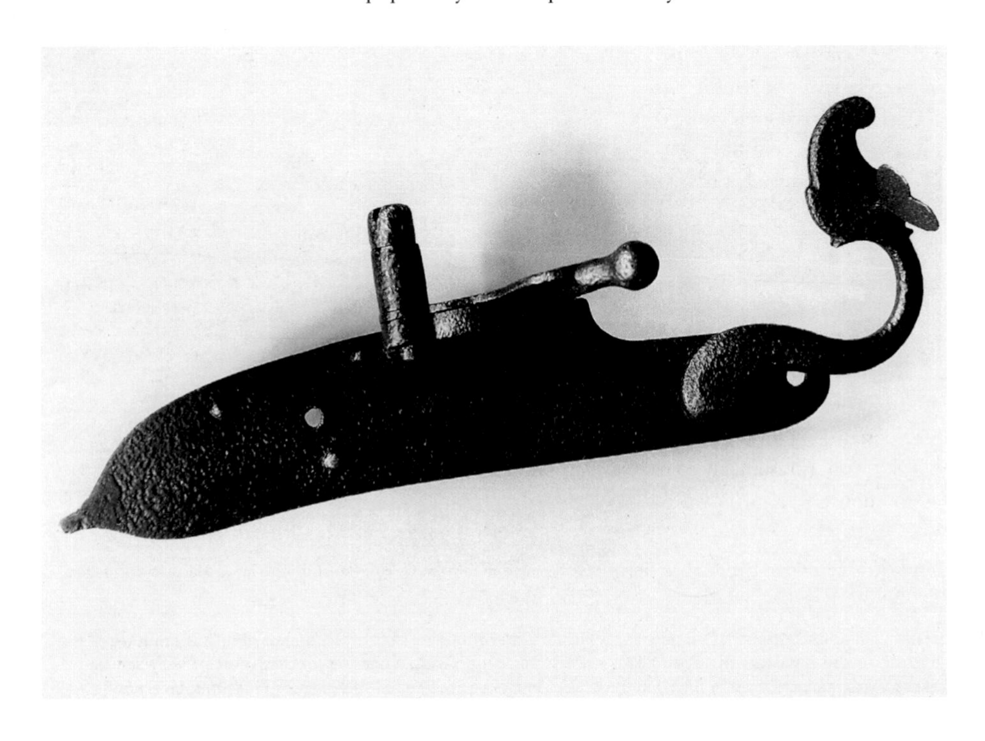

Matchlock mechanism from a musket: English(?), c.1680. This is a late military matchlock. The flash-pan is now attached to the lockplate, rather than to the barrel, and the plate itself has the contour of a contemporary flintlock mechanism.

Interior of the lock illustrated on page 8. The mechanism consists of a pivoting sear lever and its V-shaped spring. Pressure on the trigger (pinned separately to the stock) lifts the right-hand extremity of the sear, thereby depressing the left-hand end, which rotates a small tumbler to which the serpentine is attached, thus causing it to dip into the flash-pan. Releasing pressure on the trigger allows the sear spring to return the serpentine to its original position.

seventeenth century; Pierre Surirey de Saint Rémy illustrates it in his *Mémoires d'Artillerie* of 1697. In India, China and Japan, where subsequent developments in firearms ignition systems made little impact, it lasted much longer – into the nineteenth century and beyond.

Despite the sophistication of some matchlock mechanisms, all depended on smouldering matchcord in order to function. It would thus have been an advance to free the firearm from its dependence upon live fire. Present knowledge of the development of fire-making appliances is incomplete, but the common fire-steel, from which sparks are struck by a stone such as flint, is of great antiquity; Roman examples are well known. The adaptation of this device to enable it to fire a gun could have been first achieved by clamping a stone against a flat steel or rasp. When the latter was moved rapidly against the former, sparks would have been obtained to ignite the priming powder. A unique early example of a mechanism of this type is found on the so-called 'Monk's Gun' (presumably so named after Berthold Schwarz, the legendary, but fictitious, monk who was long considered to have been the inventor of gunpowder), preserved in the Historical Museum in Dresden. The age of this piece is uncertain, but it may be earlier than 1500. If the flat rasp were to have been replaced by a wheel, acting as a circular fire-steel, then a means to rotate the wheel against the stone could have been quite simply devised, thereby rendering automatic the fire-striking process. The earliest surviving self-igniting gun-locks are of this type and are termed 'wheellocks' in consequence.

Top: Barrel group from a three-shot revolving pistol: German(?), *c.*1515. This weapon, whose stock is now missing, was almost certainly fitted originally with a snap-matchlock. A comparable, and complete, pistol is in the Armoury of the Ducal Palace in Venice (no. N.30). (Ashmolean Museum, Oxford, no. 1685.B.18. Ashmolean Museum, Oxford)

Bottom: Detail of the breech of the revolver illustrated above. The flash-pans and their manually operated covers can be clearly seen. (Ashmolean Museum, Oxford)

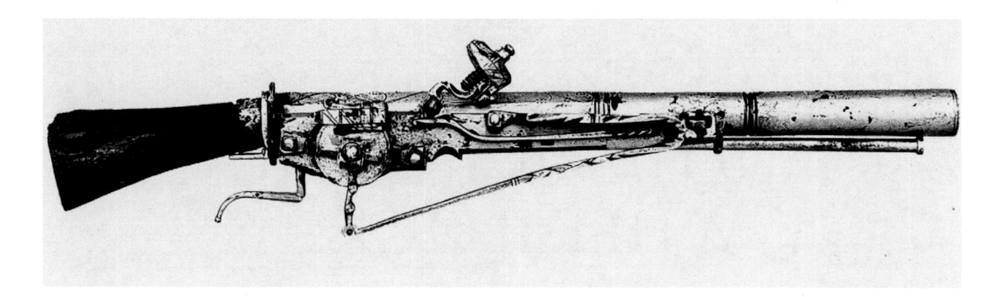

Wheellock pistol: German(?), c.1515. This is a very primitive early wheellock with a trigger and sear mechanism derived from that of the contemporary crossbow. The mainspring is mounted externally on the lockplate in front of the wheel, to which it is connected via the characteristic chain of three links. The pan cover closely resembles those fitted to the revolver illustrated opposite, but differs in that it is opened automatically when the sear is released and the wheel begins to turn. Found in a bog in Hungary in the nineteenth century, this is possibly the oldest surviving pistol. (Royal Armouries, Leeds, no. XII.1765. © The Board of Trustees of the Armouries)

Typically, a grooved wheel, protruding through a slot in the floor of the flash-pan, is connected to a V-shaped spring ('mainspring') by a chain of three links, and the spring is compressed by winding the wheel in a clockwise direction by means of a spanner applied to the squared end of its axis. Upon pulling the trigger, a lever, known as the sear (from the Latin *sera*, 'bolt'), releases the wheel, which spins rapidly through about seven-eighths of a revolution; the flash-pan cover is thrown open automatically in all but the very earliest examples. A stone (usually iron pyrites – FeS_2 – rather than flint), clamped in a small vice termed the 'dog' and pressed into the pan against the rotating wheel by a spring, produces sparks to ignite the priming powder.

The earliest reference to a wheellock was two drawings of tinder lighters in Folio 27 of the so-called *Löffelholz Manuscript*, compiled by or for the Nuremberg patrician Martin Löffelholz in 1505, and formerly preserved in the State Library in Berlin, where it was destroyed during the Second World War. The earliest reference to a (presumably) wheellock firearm appears in a book of accounts relating to expenses incurred by Cardinal Ippolito d'Este; the relevant entry is for 1507 and describes *'unam piscidem de illis que incenduntur cum lapide'* ('a gun of the type that is fired with a stone'). What are probably the earliest surviving wheellock guns are three firearms combined with crossbows (such combination weapons were not uncommon during the sixteenth century) in the Ducal Palace in Venice (nos. Q1, Q2 and Q3), which appear to have been made during the first decade of the sixteenth century. The earliest surviving complete dated piece is a pistol-carbine that formerly belonged to the Holy Roman Emperor Charles V (1519–56). It is preserved in the Royal Armoury in Madrid (no. K.32) and is dated 1530 on the barrel. It was made by the Augsburg gunmaker Bartholme Marquart. However, the precise date and place of the wheellock's invention remain unknown.

THE ERA OF THE WHEELLOCK

All Carabins or Arquebusses have wheel-works, as well those of great or small locks, which are bent with a Spanner proportionated to the thick-ness of the Axel-tree of the Wheel; upon which, when one intends to fire, he puts down the Snaphaunce, which in stead of a Flint, ought to be provided with a true Mine-stone.

Lewis de Gaya (English translation, 1678), *A Treatise of the Arms and Engines of War.*

WHEELLOCK mechanisms fall naturally into three main groups: those with an external mainspring; those with the mainspring mounted on the inner surface of the lockplate; and those in which the mainspring is housed separately in a recess cut in the mid-line of the stock.

The earliest surviving wheellocks have external mainsprings, either behind the wheel and nearest the shooter, or in front of it. From the first type evolved the lock mechanism found on the distinctive seventeenth-century Silesian birding rifles known as *Tschinkes*, and from the second arose the curious, so-called 'Portuguese' (but almost certainly south Italian) locks, which also appear to date mainly from the seventeenth century. Otherwise, locks with an external mainspring were rapidly supplanted by more sophisticated arrangements.

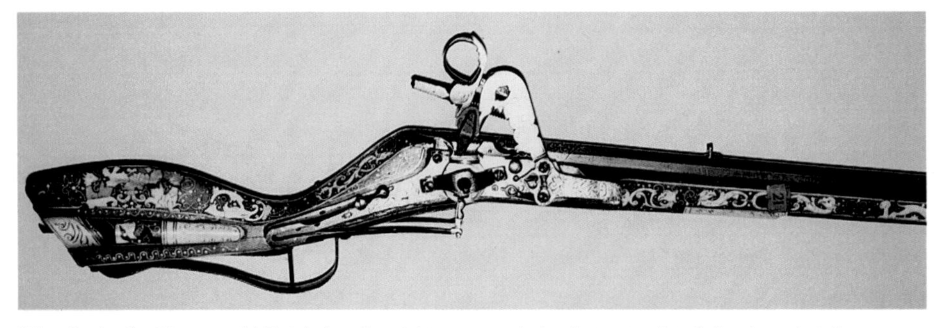

Wheellock rifle: Silesian, *c.*1645. A light rifle of this type, with the distinctive 'hind's foot' stock, is known as a *Tschinke*, the name deriving either from Teschen, the town in eastern Silesia where quantities were undoubtedly made, or from the Polish word *cienki* (pronounced 'tsiyenki'), meaning 'slender', which is certainly descriptive. (Pitt-Rivers Museum, Oxford, no. 1884.27.21)

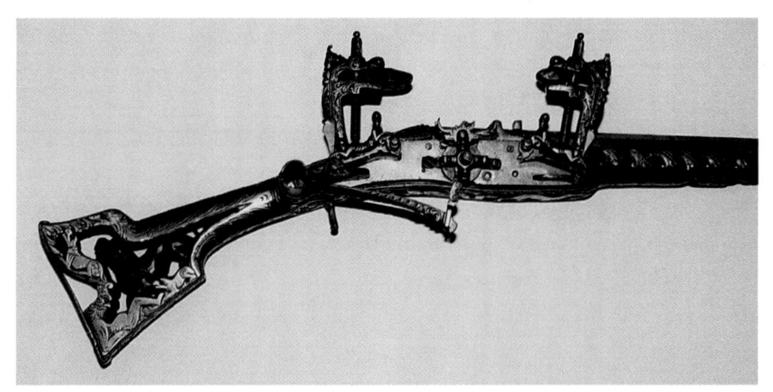

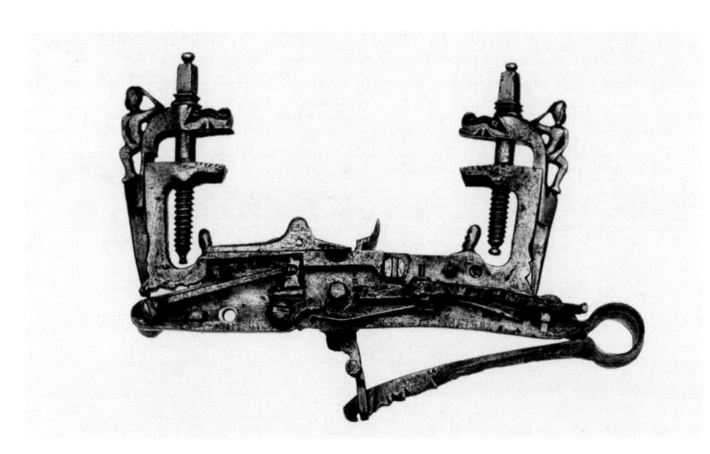

Top:
'Portuguese' wheellock: Italian (Calabria?), *c.*1650. This curious type of lock (which despite its name does not appear to have been made in Portugal) is a derivative of the kind of early wheellock illustrated on page 11.

Middle:
Wheellock gun: Italian (Sicily?), *c.*1650. The lock of this gun is clearly related to that illustrated above. Provision of a second, reserve, dog was common gunmaking practice on Italian wheellock long arms. (Liverpool Museum, no. M.4761. © National Museums, Liverpool)

Bottom:
Interior view of a similar lock to that illustrated in the middle picture. On the right can be seen the simple, one-piece sear, whose tip passes through the lockplate to hold the wheel in the spanned position. On the left can be seen the sliding pan cover and its arm; a cam (missing) on the wheel axis automatically opens the cover when the wheel begins to turn. (Royal Armouries, Leeds, no. XII.1581. © The Board of Trustees of the Armouries)

Right: Interior of wheellock: German, c.1535. This is an early example of a fully developed standard wheellock, in which the principal mechanical parts are mounted on the inner surface of the lockplate. To the right is the V-shaped mainspring, with its lower arm hooked onto the chain attached to the wheel axis. This last is supported by a bracket, or bridle, which is screwed to the lockplate. Between the arms of the mainspring is the sear mechanism – a two-component assembly, as in the majority of wheellocks. To the left can be seen the pan cover and its arm, again activated by a cam on the wheel axis. (Royal Armouries, Leeds, no. XII.1566. © The Board of Trustees of the Armouries)

Wheellocks with an internal mainspring are the commonest type and may consequently be considered the standard design. The earliest surviving evidence for such an arrangement is to be found in Folio 56 of the *Codex Atlanticus* of Leonardo da Vinci, where a wheellock for a gun is illustrated. The date of the manuscript is not known with certainty, but it must be earlier than 1519, the year of Leonardo's death. The earliest actual example of such a lock is that on a combined crossbow and gun in the Bavarian National Museum in Munich (no. W.1498); this piece bears a coat of arms used by the Archduke Ferdinand of Austria only between the years 1521 and 1526.

The third type of wheellock, in which the mainspring is detached from the lockplate and housed in a separate slot in the stock, is generally regarded as being specifically French. It probably represents a primitive arrangement, derived from crossbow constructional practice (in which all the mechanical parts are mounted in a recess in the mid-line of the stock), which found

Below: Wheellock: German, c.1550. In this lock the dog spring encircles the wheel like a sickle blade, an arrangement particularly associated with the city of Nuremberg; it fell from use after about 1560. To the left of the wheel can be seen a safety catch that blocks the sear. (Royal Armouries, Leeds, no. XII.43. © The Board of Trustees of the Armouries)

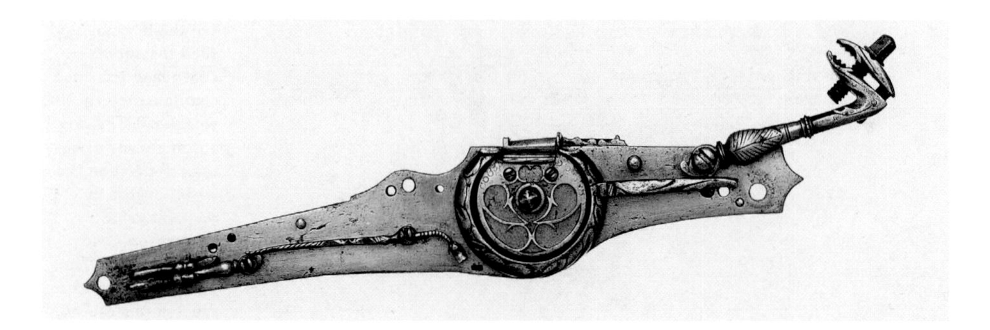

particular favour in France. The earliest known example, which may not itself be French, is on a short gun in the Army Museum in Paris (no. M.Po.794), which probably dates from *c.*1525.

By the end of the fifteenth century a characteristic form of gunstock had evolved from the tiller of the primitive hand-gun. Influenced by the stock of the contemporary crossbow, and intended to be held over the shoulder and

Above: Detail of wheellock pistol: Flemish(?), *c.*1560. The metal parts of this pistol are inlaid with gold and silver. The arms of the dog spring are of unequal length, the upper being the longer. This arrangement seems to have originated in Augsburg in Germany and thence spread to the Low Countries, Spain and Italy. Elsewhere, spring arms of equal length were favoured (cf. middle picture, page 17). The dog is in the forward, 'safe', position, clear of the wheel. (Royal Armouries, Leeds, no. XII.10250. © The Board of Trustees of the Armouries)

Wheellock: Italian (Tuscany), *c.*1620. Most early-seventeenth-century Italian firearms are associated with the city of Brescia in Lombardy. This superb lock is an exception, bearing the mark of the Florentine maker Gian Parigin. (Pitt-Rivers Museum, Oxford, no. 1884.27.25)

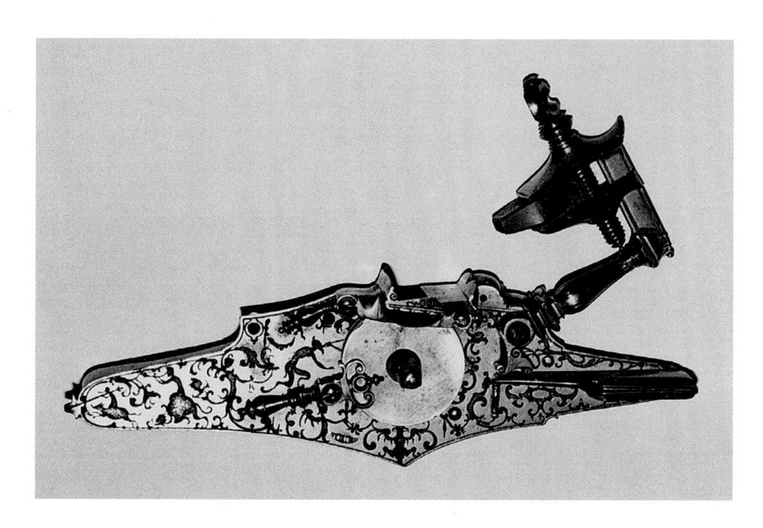

against the cheek during firing, it was the earliest form of the *deutsche Schaft*, or German cheek-stock. It was to enjoy a lasting popularity in Germany and Austria until the end of the wheellock era, although after the beginning of the seventeenth century its use was largely confined to rifles. To the south and west of the German-speaking area a variety of stock types evolved during the sixteenth century that were intended to be held against the shoulder in the modern way, and by the end of the century such patterns were employed also in Germany on carbines and other military long arms.

The invention of the wheellock stimulated the development of the pistol (European matchlock pistols are almost unknown). A variety of styles emerged during the first half of the sixteenth century, to be largely

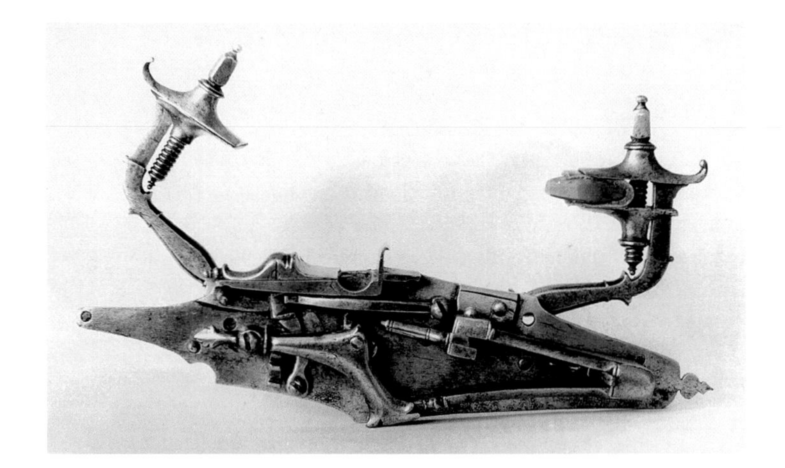

Interior of wheellock: Italian, *c.*1650. This is a typically elegant Brescian product. The Italian liking for a second dog is again apparent.

Detail of wheellock pistol: Spanish (Catalonia), *c.*1615. This pistol (a so-called *pedreñal*) is an early product of the Catalan gunmaking centre of Ripoll, where pistols (especially) of a distinctive and archaic character continued to be manufactured into the nineteenth century. The dog (with its stone) is set down on the closed pan cover; primed and with the wheel spanned, the pistol would be ready to fire. (National Museums of Scotland, Edinburgh, no. 1874.1.31. © The Trustees of the National Museums of Scotland)

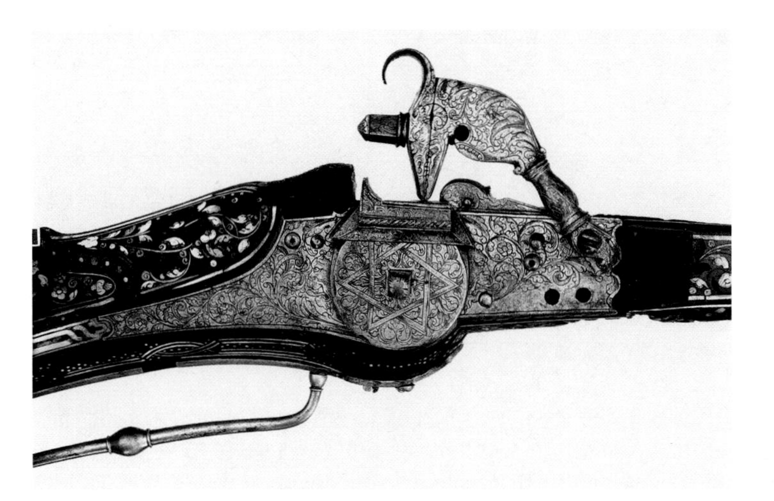

Detail of wheellock gun: French, *c.*1580. The mainspring is mounted in the characteristic French manner, detached from the lockplate and housed in a slot in the mid-line of the stock. (Royal Armouries, Leeds, no. XII.1441. © The Board of Trustees of the Armouries)

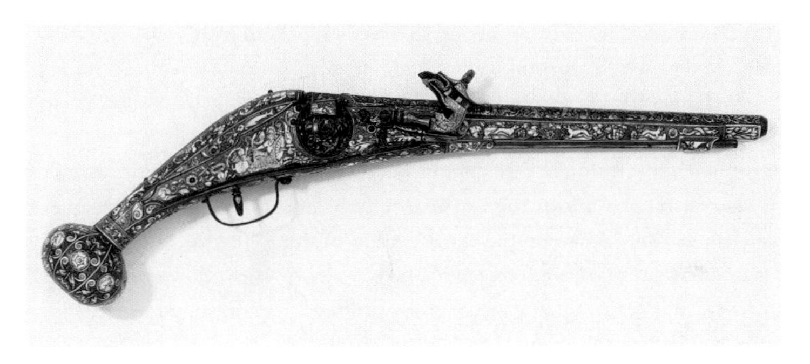

Wheellock pistol: English, *c.*1585. This magnificent pistol, its metal parts damascened in gold and silver, is the only known sixteenth-century English wheellock. Traditionally made for Sir William Harris of Shenfield House, Margaretting, Essex, it was preserved for several centuries at Belchamp Hall in Essex. (Victoria and Albert Museum, London, no. M.949.1983. V&A Images/ Victoria and Albert Museum, London)

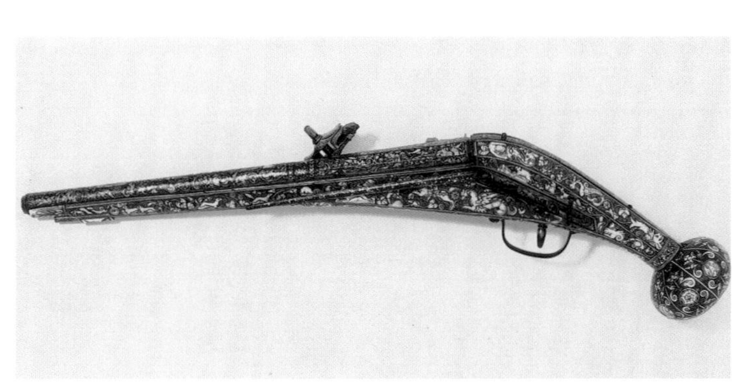

Left-hand side of the same pistol. A small metal plate bears a long belt-hook and a safety-catch mechanism operating on an extension of the sear. Apart from its being English, this is otherwise a typical ball-butted pistol of the last quarter of the sixteenth century. (V&A Images/Victoria and Albert Museum, London)

Detail of breech-loading gun: English(?), dated 1537. This target gun was made for King Henry VIII (reigned 1509–47); its original wheellock is now missing. The hinged breech-block, operating on the snuff-box principle, is shown open. Stylistically, the weapon suggests a maker originating from the Low Countries; his initials, 'WH', are stamped on the barrel. (Royal Armouries, Leeds, no. XII.1. © The Board of Trustees of the Armouries)

superseded after about 1565 by a distinctive type of butt terminating in a spherical pommel. These ball-butted pistols are termed *Puffer* in Germany, although their use was not confined to that country as this was very much an international style. During the early years of the succeeding century the ball-butt became ovoid, and after about 1620 it disappeared from fashionable use, being replaced by a graceful, flaring style of butt, lacking a separate pommel.

With the principal exceptions of Italy and Spain, stock decoration during the sixteenth century typically took the form of a profuse inlay of engraved bone, with the frequent addition in north-western and eastern Europe of mother-of-pearl. Outside the German cultural area, this scheme of ornament had fallen from favour by the third decade of the following century, being replaced by a preference for plain (usually walnut) or exotic wood, polished to reveal the grain. Inlay was generally limited to a restrained use of silver wire, and more attention was paid to the increasingly substantial metal mounts (butt-cap, trigger-guard, ramrod pipes) constituting the stock furniture. Apart from wood, other materials were sometimes employed for stocking, notably ivory (in Holland), and brass and iron (in Scotland, Germany and Italy).

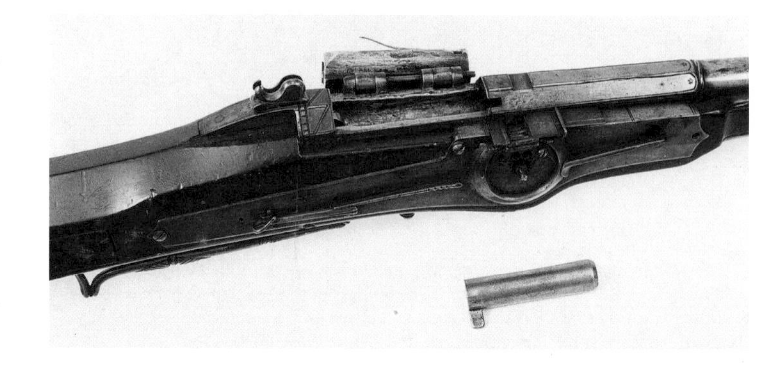

Detail of breech-loading gun: German, *c.*1550. Slightly later in date than the piece illustrated above, this gun retains its self-spanning wheellock (but not the dog) and has a reloadable chamber. (Rotunda Museum, Woolwich, no. IX.5. Courtesy of the Royal Artillery Historical Trust)

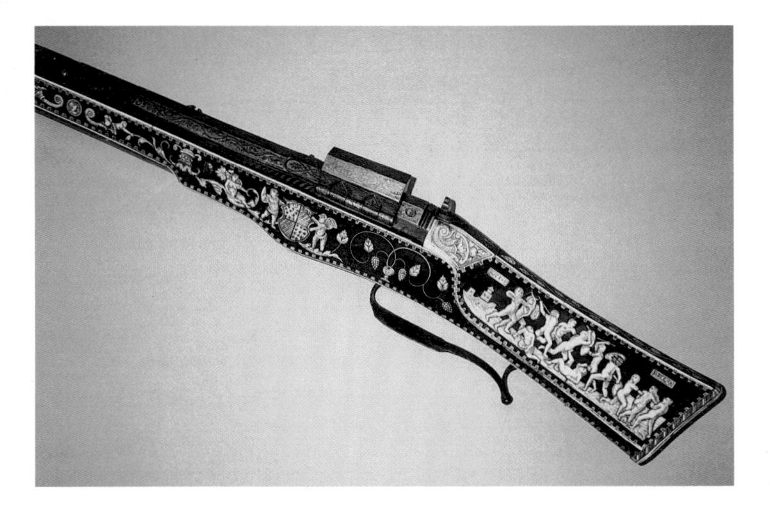

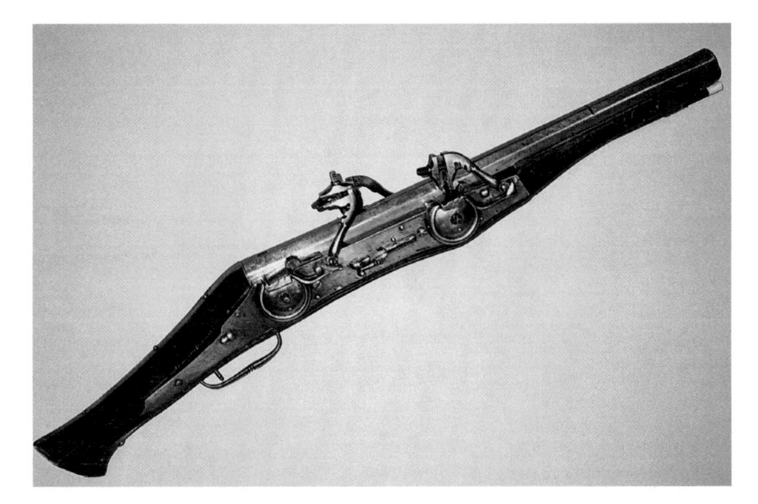

Top:
Wheellock gun: German, *c.*1550. This is another breech-loading gun working on the snuff-box principle. This view shows the cheek piece of the typical German-style butt. The scene depicted in engraved bone inlay is the abduction of Helen of Troy. (Kelvingrove Museum, Glasgow, no. 1939.65.un. Photography allowed by kind permission of Glasgow Museums)

Bottom:
Three-shot superimposed-load wheellock pistol: German, *c.*1555. The style of butt is typical for the period. The three superimposed charges are fired one after the other by three lock mechanisms, two on the right-hand side of the pistol, and one on the left. (Kelvingrove Museum, Glasgow, no. 1939.65.zg. Photography allowed by kind permission of Glasgow Museums)

Attempts were continually made to improve the accuracy, and to increase the firing rate, of hand firearms. Front and rear sights are illustrated in a 1471 manuscript by Martin Mertz of Amberg, *Kunst aus Buchsen zu Schiessen* ('Art of Shooting out of Guns'), preserved in the Bavarian State Library (CGM.599). Rifling – spiral grooves (typically six or seven) cut into the bore of the barrel and which impart to the bullet in flight a spinning motion, and hence gyroscopic stability – appears to have been a German invention of the first half of the sixteenth century. The earliest dated example known is a barrel of 1542, mounted on a later gun, preserved in the Royal Danish Arsenal Museum in Copenhagen (no. B.277).

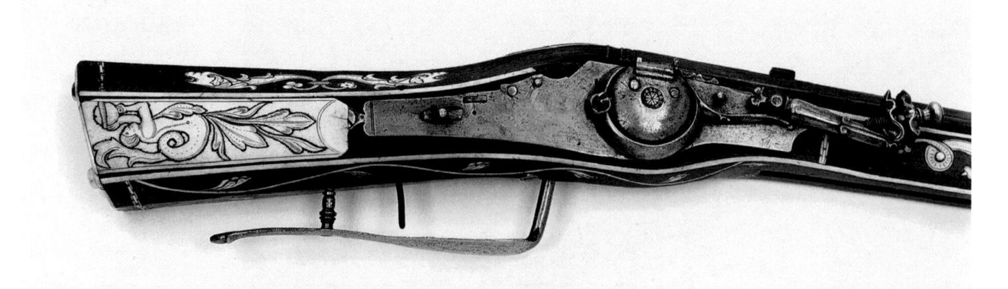

Wheellock gun: German, *c.*1550. This is a typical German gun of the mid sixteenth century. The lock is unusual, however, in that it is geared; thus the wheel makes more than two revolutions, instead of the usual three-quarters or seven-eighths turn. There is a butt-trap (a so-called 'patch box') with a sliding cover immediately behind the lock – a feature particularly associated with rifles, wheellock or otherwise. (Birmingham Museum, no. 1885.S.00041. Birmingham Museums and Art Gallery and V&A Images/Victoria and Albert Museum, London)

Powder horn: German, *c.*1580. The body is made of stag's antler.

Iron powder flask: Italian, *c.*1600.

To secure a higher rate of fire, two avenues were explored. In the first, to accelerate the process of loading, various breech-loading mechanisms were tried. In the second, attempts were made to increase the number of shots that could be fired before reloading became necessary.

The commonest breech-loading arrangement encountered on wheellock firearms is that working on the so-called 'snuff-box' principle. In this, there

is a hinged breech-block which, when opened to the side like the lid of a box, permits the insertion of a previously loaded metal chamber in a manner similar to that of a modern cartridge. Wheellock firearms with this type of breech mechanism generally have self-spanning locks in which the dog is linked to the wheel, either by gear wheels or by a chain, thereby dispensing with the need for a separate spanner – movement of the dog being all that is required to wind up the wheel. The earliest surviving gun of the snuff-box type is one made for King Henry VIII of England (1509–47) in 1537; it is preserved in the Royal Armouries in Leeds (no. XII.1; page 18).

The most basic approach to a multiple-shot weapon was simply to increase the number of barrels, although considerations of weight imposed limitations on such designs. The barrels could be either fixed or revolving, the latter system having the advantage of requiring only one lock mechanism. Examples of both types survive from the early sixteenth century; the remains of a three-barrelled revolving pistol or short gun of *c.*1515 is preserved in the Ashmolean Museum in Oxford (no. 1685.B.18; figures page 10).

Left: Spanner for wheellock: German(?), *c.*1640. The spanner – for three sizes of wheel axis – is combined with an adjustable powder measure.

Below: Wheellock pistol: English(?), *c.*1640. This pistol was found wrapped in a piece of yellow Spanish brocade under the floorboards of the south-west bedroom of the Governor's House in Bridgnorth, Shropshire. The stock is crudely incised with the initials 'RH' – probably for Sir Robert Howard of Clun, who was the Royalist governor of Bridgnorth during the English Civil War. The town surrendered to Parliamentary forces on 26th April 1646. The pistol is otherwise a typical military piece of the period, of an international design.

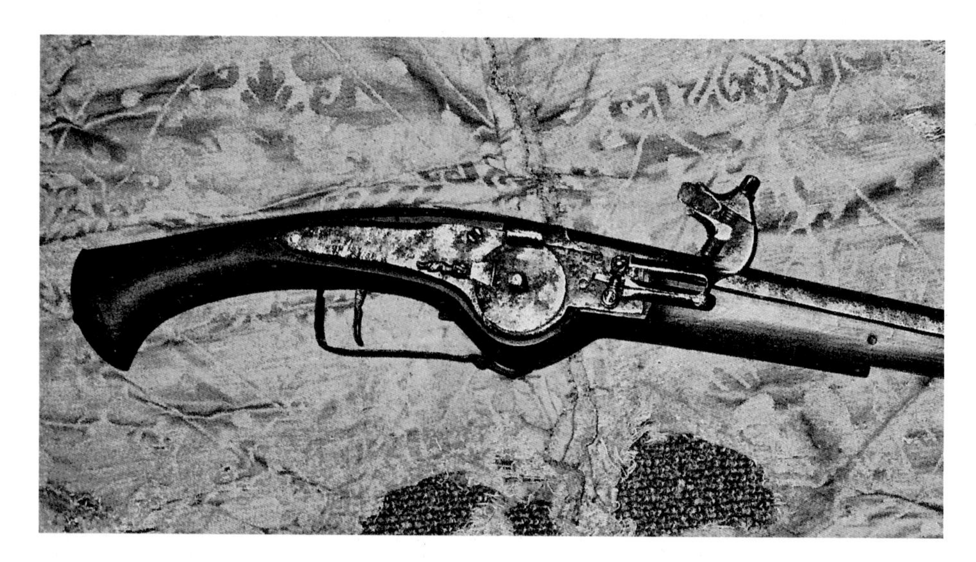

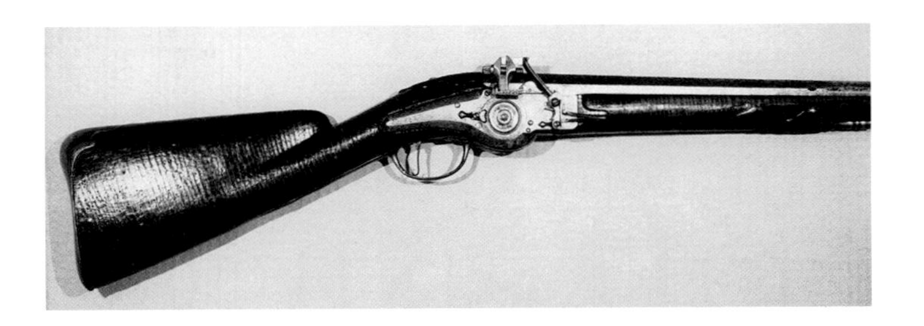

Wheellock gun: English, *c.*1700. This unusual sporting gun has a self-spanning lock. It was made by the prominent Warwick gunmaker Nicholas Paris. (Warwickshire Museum, no. H.2543. By kind permission of Warwickshire Museum Service)

Various types of magazine weapon were also developed, some of great complexity. The simplest of these were those of the superimposed-load variety, in which the barrel itself acted as the magazine. A number of charges, most commonly two, were loaded one on top of the other and were then fired off one after the other, typically using the appropriate number of lock mechanisms. The danger was of simultaneous multiple discharge, but with a two-shot weapon this was probably of small consequence, and repeating firearms on this principle were made in considerable quantities until the middle of the nineteenth century.

The wheellock fell from favour in most of Europe during the second half of the seventeenth century, the main reasons for this probably being its relative complexity, the need for a separate spanner, and its tendency to jam if kept wound up for any length of time. It continued to be made in parts of the German-speaking area, especially Austria, until well after 1800; a detached lock signed *Dasch in Gratz*, and dating from 1810, is in the Joanneum Museum in Graz (no. KG.21407). The manufacture of wheellocks was almost entirely confined to Europe, although imported locks were certainly used in Turkey, and examples of singular construction appear to have been made in Japan during the early nineteenth century.

THE DEVELOPMENT OF THE FLINTLOCK

... but when a Musket is to be shot off, then such a Motion being applied to the Trigger by virtue of the contrivance of the Engin, the spring is immediately let loos, the Cock fals down, and knocks the Flint against the Steel, opens the Pan, strikes fire upon the Powder in it, which by the Touch-hole fires the Powder in the Barrel, and that with great noise throws out the ponderous leaden bullet ...

Robert Boyle (1664), *Usefullnesse of Experimental Natural Philosophy.*

Snaphaunce gun: Savoyard, c.1580. The unusual lock fitted to this gun is closely related to those on the four earliest dated (1571 and 1572) snaphaunce weapons. The lockplate is stamped with a maker's mark attributed to Jacques Robert, who was court gunmaker to Carlo Emanuele I (1580–1630), Duke of Savoy. (Pitt-Rivers Museum, Oxford, no. 1884.27.27)

AT some time before the middle of the sixteenth century another type of fire-striking lock appeared. This was the earliest of a group of mechanisms generally termed flintlocks, and these imitate the action of striking sparks manually from a domestic fire-steel. A piece of flint is clamped in the vice-like jaws of a cock (so called from its pecking motion), which is pulled back against the pressure of a mainspring until it is held by the sear. On pulling the trigger, the sear is disengaged, the cock snaps forward and in so doing causes the flint to strike a pivoted and spring-controlled fire-steel, or 'frizzen', which is thereby flung forward in its turn, exposing the flash-pan to the resultant shower of sparks. A distinction is usually made between those

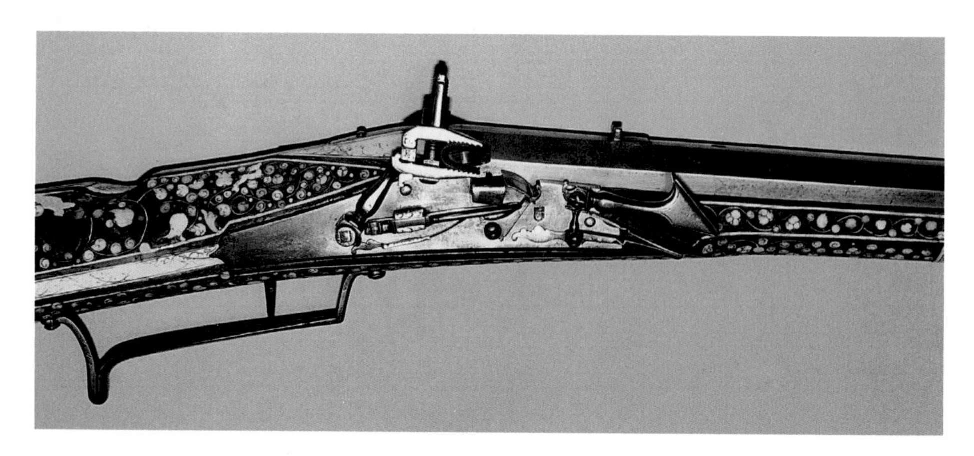

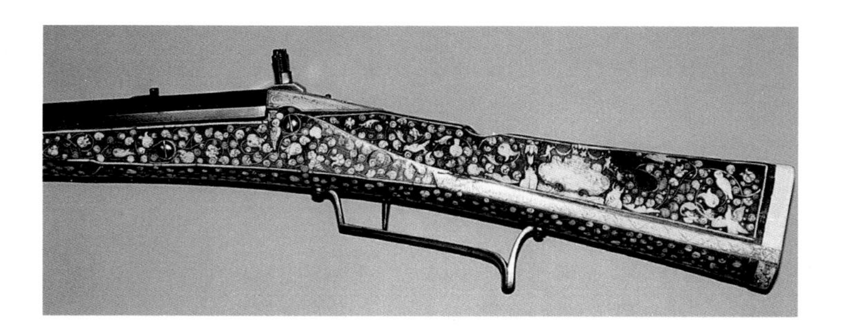

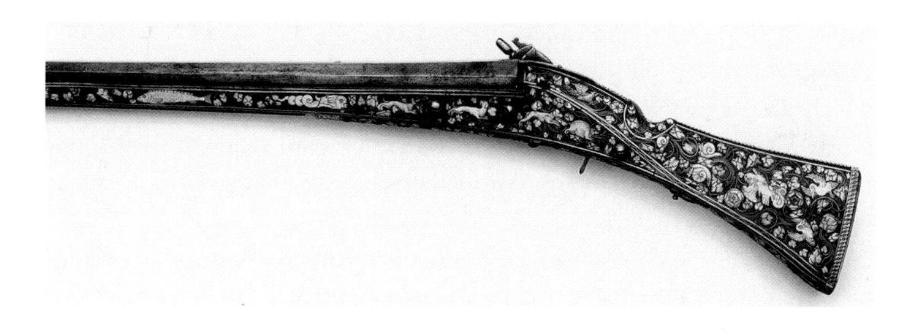

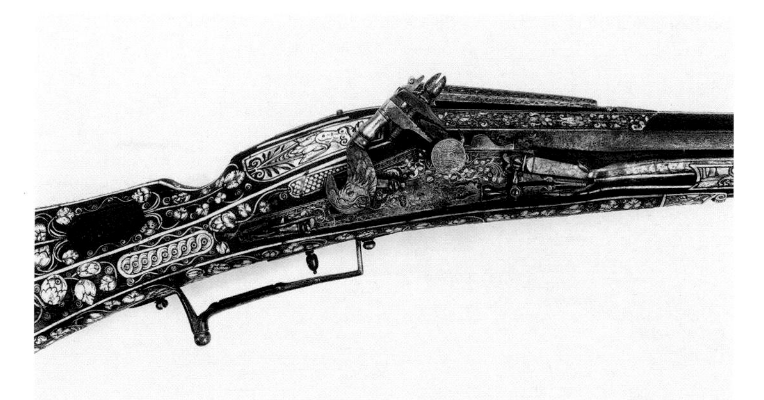

Illustrations, from top to bottom:

Left-hand view of the gun illustrated on page 24.

Snaphaunce gun: English, dated 1588. This gun was originally at Belchamp Hall in Essex (cf. page 17). The barrel bears a maker's mark 'RA' – possibly for Richard Assomes of London. The stock is inlaid with engraved bone, comprising panels linked by tendrils with fishes, birds, snails, flowers, and other motifs found on contemporary English textiles. The frizzen is missing; a safety catch of wheellock type, operating on the sear, is situated behind the cock. (Victoria and Albert Museum, London, no. M.948.1983. V&A Images/Victoria and Albert Museum, London)

Left-hand side of the gun illustrated above. (V&A Images/Victoria and Albert Museum, London)

Detail of snaphaunce gun: English, dated 1590. (Royal Armouries, Leeds, no. XII.1785. © The Board of Trustees of the Armouries)

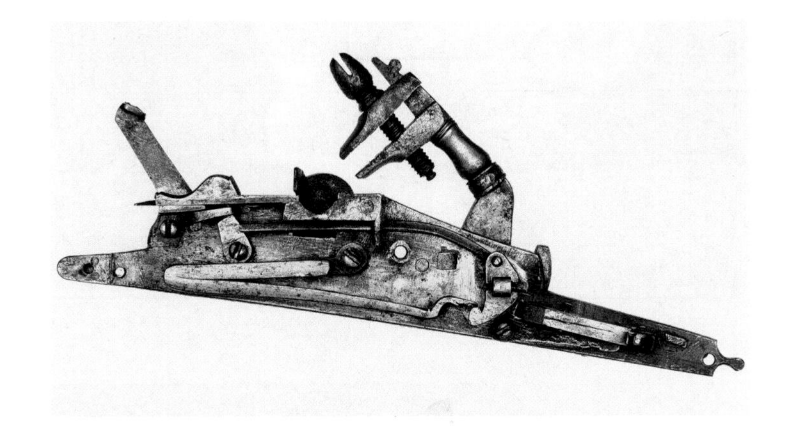

Interior of the lock of the gun illustrated on page 25 (bottom). To the left is the V-shaped mainspring bearing on the tumbler, which is fixed to the inner end of the cock axis. To the tumbler is linked the push-rod, which opens the sliding pan cover of wheellock type when the cock falls; the pan-cover assembly can be seen above the short upper arm of the mainspring. On the right, behind the tumbler, is the two-piece sear of wheellock type which engages the tail of the cock when this is pulled back. (© The Board of Trustees of the Armouries)

(generally earlier) locks in which the flash-pan cover is a separate entity, and those in which it is combined with the frizzen to form a single L-shaped unit. Since the nineteenth century the archaic term 'snaphaunce' has been applied to the former group, and this usage will be followed here.

The early history of the flintlock is more obscure than that of the wheellock. There seems little doubt that the earliest mechanisms were those that would nowadays be called snaphaunces, and the earliest survivor is probably a gun in the Royal Armouries in Stockholm (no. LRK.16317), which almost certainly dates from 1556. The earliest dated pieces are four nearly identical muskets, marked either 1571 or 1572 on their barrels; one of 1572 in the Veste Coburg Museum (no. IV.D.117) may be taken as representative of the group.

The majority of snaphaunce weapons fall naturally into three main groups: Scandinavian-Baltic, Anglo-Scottish, and Italian.

The Scandinavian group includes the most primitive, and therefore perhaps the oldest, examples; the earliest locks have external mainsprings (cf.

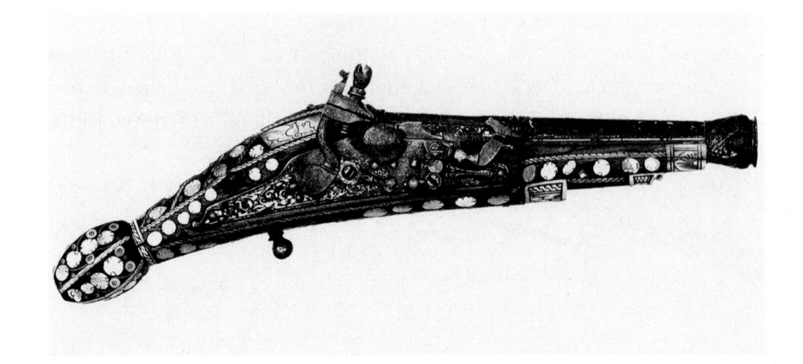

Snaphaunce pistol: English, c.1605. The iron parts are inlaid with gold and silver, the stock with bone and mother-of-pearl. A bulbous trigger without a trigger guard was a commonplace arrangement on small English pistols of the seventeenth century. (Royal Armouries, Leeds, no. XII.1823. © The Board of Trustees of the Armouries)

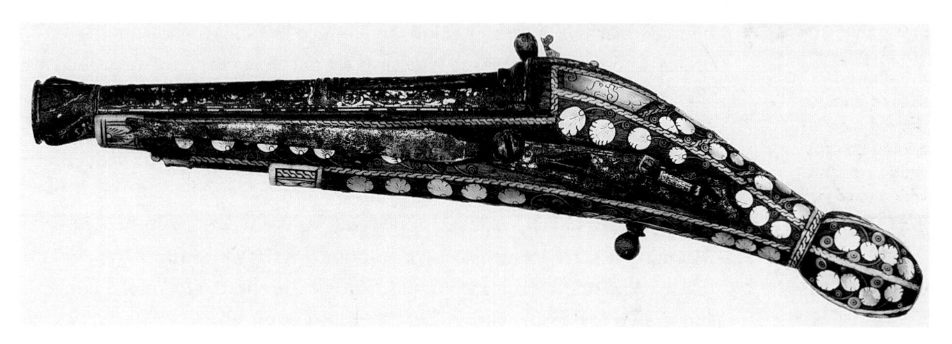

Top: Snaphaunce mechanism: English, c.1630. This mechanism has a 'dog' safety catch – an unusual feature on a snaphaunce. It is shown engaged with the tail of the cock.

Bottom: Left-hand side of the pistol illustrated opposite. A metal plate bears a belt-hook and a safety-catch mechanism (cf. bottom picture, page 17). (© The Board of Trustees of the Armouries)

wheellocks). The transformation into a lock with a combined frizzen and flash-pan cover seems to have occurred relatively early, and in such cases the frizzen is typically pivoted on the pan cover with a screw, which enables it to be rotated out of the way of the cock with the pan cover closed – a useful safety arrangement in a lock lacking a separate pan cover. The cocks on these locks all tend to be elongated, and frequently angular. One variety of Russian snaphaunce has affinities with this group.

Locks of Anglo-Scottish type were also manufactured in Holland, Russia and Morocco. All have an internal mainspring working on a tumbler fixed to the inner end of the cock axis; a block of metal, or 'buffer', screwed to the exterior of the lockplate to arrest the fall of the cock; and the distinctive feature of a prominent button, or 'fence', on the outer border of the flash-pan. On Scottish examples the fence frequently bears a date, the earliest being 1598 on a pair of pistols in the Historical Museum in Dresden (nos. 1431 and 1432). Seventeenth-century Scottish long arms are exceptionally rare, pistols less so. The earliest ones are stocked in brazil wood, but increasingly the tendency was to use either brass or iron, brass being the

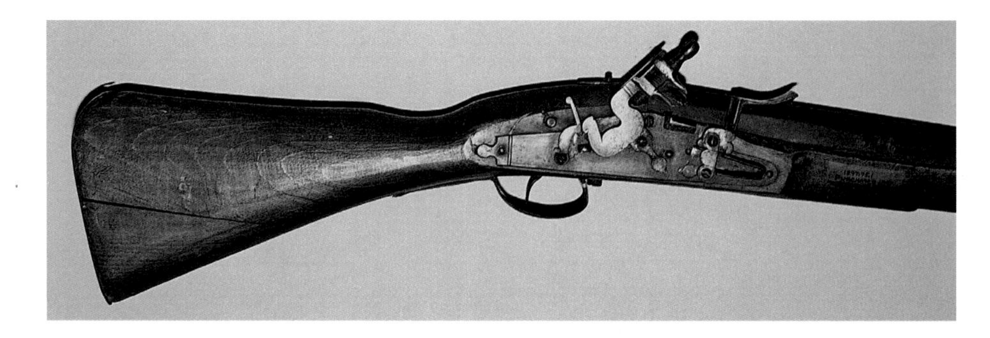

Musket with so-called 'English flintlock': English, c.1650. The pan cover and frizzen are now combined in a single L-shaped unit. A dog-catch is visible behind the cock. (Pitt-Rivers Museum, Oxford, no. 1897.75.1)

commoner during the early seventeenth century. The pistols can be classified according to the shape of the butt: either a graceful 'fishtail', or an ovoid 'lemon' pommel. From the early part of the century, such weapons typically bear the marks of makers working in Dundee or Edinburgh; from the 1660s onwards, provincial centres – famously Doune in Perthshire – predominate. The earliest dated English snaphaunce is a gun of 1584 in the National Museum in Copenhagen (no. 10428). At some time around 1630 the separate pan cover was done away with in England to produce the so-called 'English flintlock', which remained very popular until around 1670. Such locks generally have a half-cock safety position on the sear, in common with the majority of mechanisms having a combined frizzen and pan cover. English locks frequently have an additional safety feature in the form of a hook, or 'dog-catch', to secure the cock in the half-cock position.

Interior of a lock similar to that on the gun illustrated above. The mainspring can be seen to the left, its lower arm bearing on the tumbler. The one-piece sear can be seen to the right; this engages with the tumbler to provide the half-cock (safety) position, and with the tail of the cock externally for full-cock. The lock is shown in the 'fired' configuration, with the cock down, the frizzen forward, and the flash-pan uncovered. (Liverpool Museum, no. M.4761. © National Museums, Liverpool)

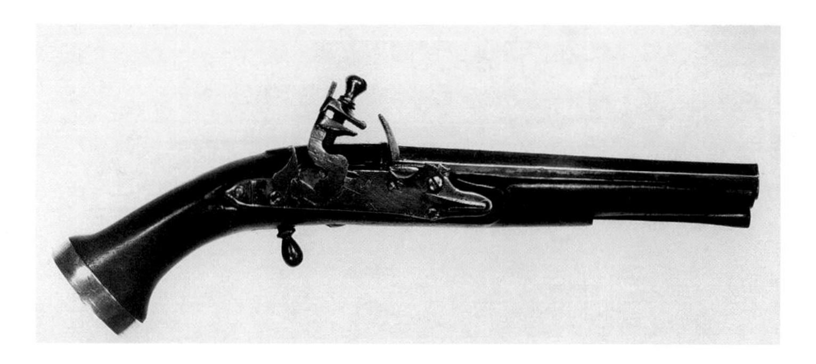

Top: English lock pistol: English, c.1645. The lockplate and barrel are both of brass; this is another pocket pistol (cf. bottom picture, page 26 and bottom picture, page 43). The cock is at half-cock, with the dog-catch engaged and the frizzen covering the flash-pan. The pistol would be carried in this state, the cock being pulled back to the full-cock position before firing. (Kelvingrove Museum, Glasgow, no. 1939.65.aam. Glasgow City Council Museums)

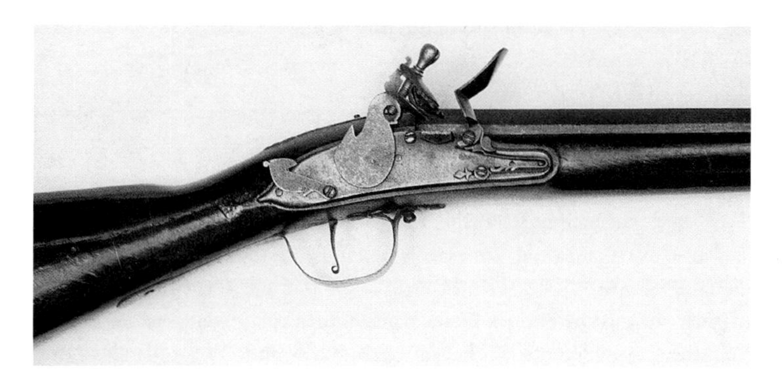

Middle: Detail of English lock musket: English, c.1670. The lock on this weapon is a later version of the English flintlock. It has a more sophisticated appearance, and both the half- and full-cock positions are taken on the tumbler inside the lock. (Courtesy of Wallis & Wallis)

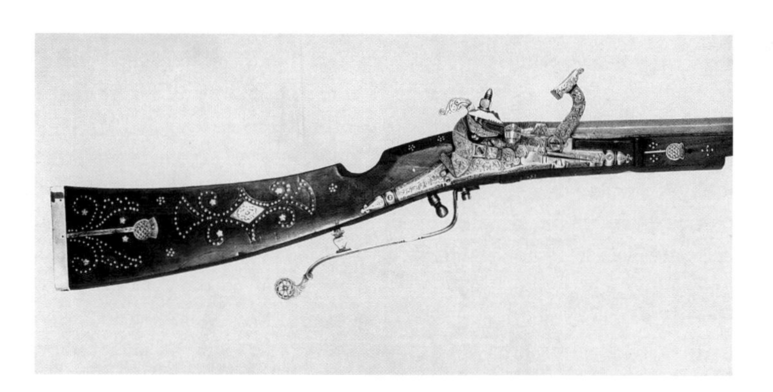

Snaphaunce gun: Scottish, dated 1614. Scottish long arms of traditional form are rare, fewer than thirty having survived. The brazil-wood stock of this small gun, which once belonged to King Louis XIII of France (1610–43), is inlaid with silver; the lockplate is of gilt brass. It bears the maker's mark attributed to Robert Alison of Dundee. (Royal Armouries, Leeds, no. XII.63. © The Board of Trustees of the Armouries)

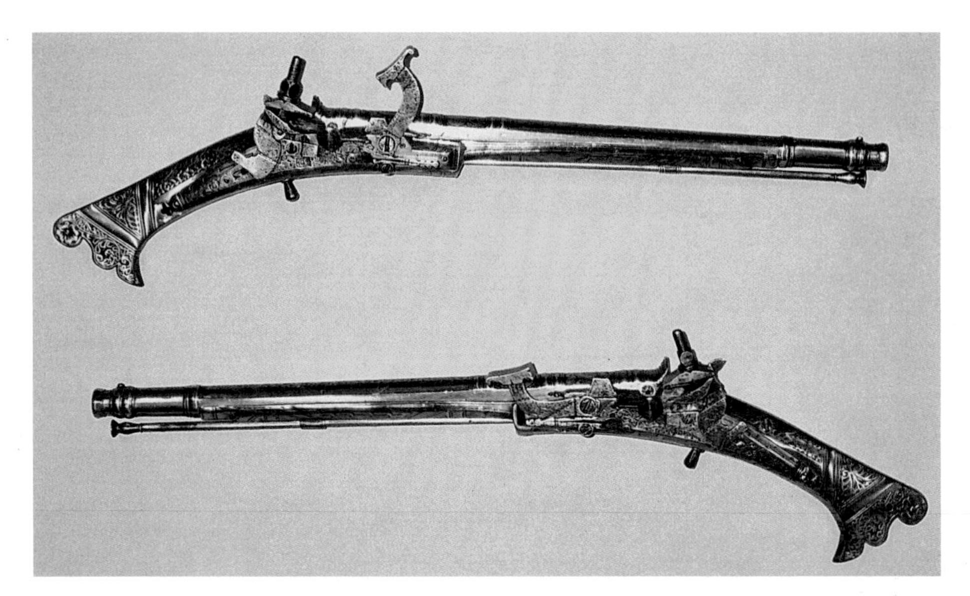

Pair of snaphaunce pistols: Scottish, dated 1624 and 1626. This is a typically elegant pair of brass-stocked, fishtail-butted Scottish pistols; the locks are dated 1624, and the barrels 1626. They are provided with right- and left-handed locks, which was standard practice on pistols made in Scotland at this time. They bear the maker's mark attributed to James Low of Dundee. (Kelvingrove Museum, Glasgow, nos. 1940.45.h and i. Photography allowed by kind permission of Glasgow Museums)

The snaphaunce in Italy (the 'Florentine' lock) was generally of a very elegant construction and was especially popular in the central regions from the late seventeenth century through to the mid nineteenth. The town of Anghiari in Tuscany was particularly prominent as a manufacturing centre from the mid eighteenth century onwards. Locks were frequently dated, the latest recorded being 1845.

Snaphaunce weapons appear never to have been made in either Spain or Portugal, where locks with a combined frizzen and pan cover were apparently being manufactured as early as the sixteenth century. What is probably the oldest surviving example – almost certainly dating from before 1600 – is a double-barrelled combined pistol and lance in the Royal Armoury in Madrid (no. I.20). The classic Spanish flintlock has an external mainspring that presses upwards on the heel of the cock; half- and full-cock sears protrude through the lockplate to engage a little foot on the cock to hold it respectively in the safety and firing positions. This little foot gives the lock its Spanish name of *patilla*, although such mechanisms tend to be referred to nowadays as 'miquelet' locks. *Patilla* locks were also popular outside Spain itself, being manufactured in Portugal, southern Italy, the Balkans, Turkey, Persia and the Caucasus. Similar miquelet locks were also popular in central Italy. These, too, have an external mainspring, but in these so-called 'Roman' locks the spring presses downwards on the toe of the cock, in contrast to the Spanish arrangement. Related mechanisms were made in Catalonia and Algeria. The rarest variety of miquelet lock is that associated with Portugal, the *fecho de molinhas* ('spring lock'). This is distinguished by its having the

Snaphaunce pistol: Italian, *c.*1645–50. A very characterful snaphaunce lock is mounted on an otherwise typical, albeit long – 29 inches (74 cm) – north Italian pistol dating from just before the middle of the seventeenth century. The pierced and engraved iron butt-cap and trigger guard are fine Brescian work of the period. The barrel is signed 'GIO. BATT. FRANCI.' for Giovan Battista Francino, who was the second of five successive family members of that name who worked in the barrel-making centre of Gardone Val Trompia, ten miles to the north of Brescia. (Pitt-Rivers Museum, Oxford, no. 1884.27.76)

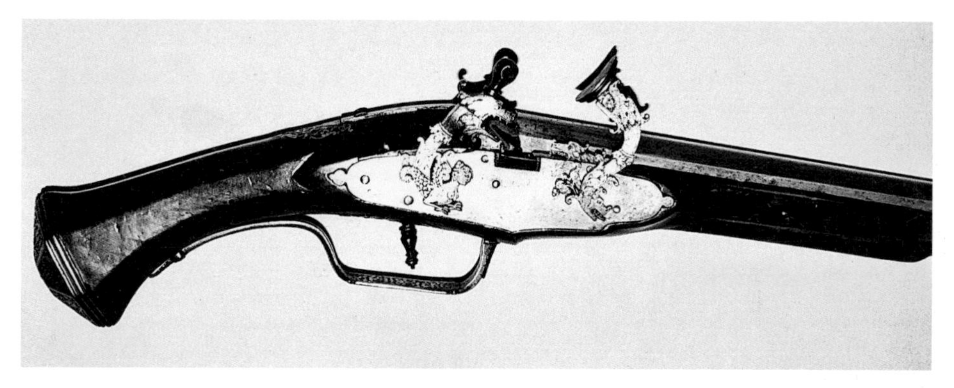

Patilla miquelet lock: Turkish, eighteenth century. Mechanically, this silver-damascened lock is a typical miquelet of Spanish type with the mainspring pressing upwards on the heel of the cock. The ring terminal to the upper jaw screw of the cock is an almost invariable feature on miquelet locks of all types.

Top: 'Roman' miquelet lock: Italian, dated 1735. A miquelet lock of central Italian type, in which the mainspring presses down on the toe of the cock. It is signed 'Vittorio Sagnotti'; the maker appears to have worked in Rome itself.

Middle: Miquelet lock *a la moda*: Spanish, late eighteenth century. The *a la moda* lock combines the elegant external appearance of the French flintlock with the laterally operating sears of the Spanish miquelet lock, which pass through the lockplate to engage the cock; the earliest known example dates from 1697. The lock illustrated was made in Placencia about one hundred years later than this and is a rare military version from a light infantry musket.

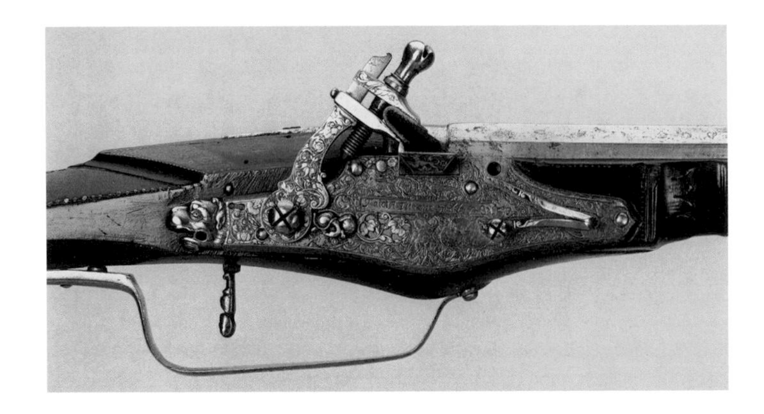

Bottom: Detail of flintlock gun: French, dated 1630. This is the earliest known flintlock of French type with a vertically pivoting sear. The lockplate is signed 'Faict. A. Turene. m. d. l.'. (Windsor Castle, no. L.316. The Royal Collection © 2007 Her Majesty Queen Elizabeth II)

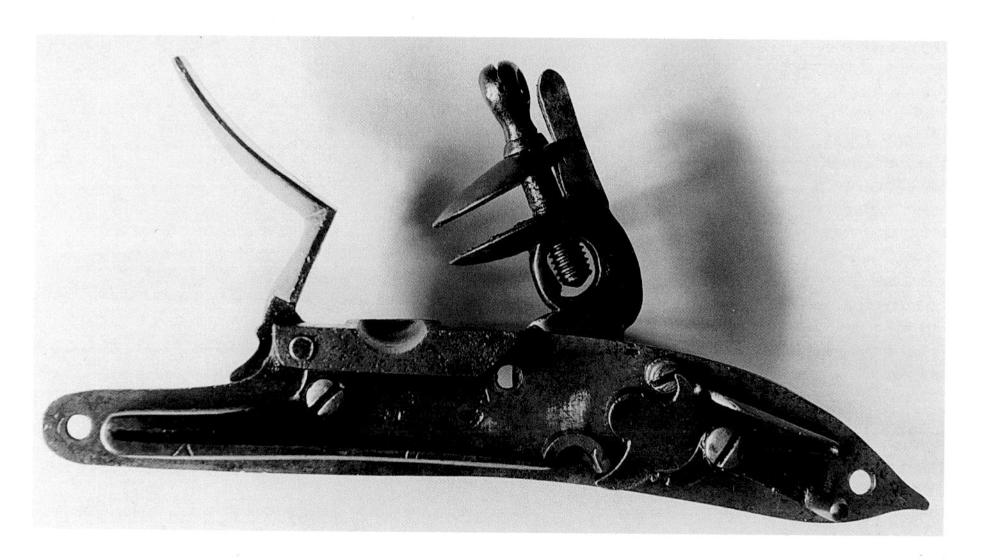

Interior of flintlock: English, dated 174(?). This is a basic flintlock. To the left is the mainspring, bearing on the tumbler, which is engaged in its half- and full-cock notches by the vertically pivoting sear visible to its right. The lock is in the 'fired' configuration.

more conventional arrangement of an internal mainspring – as does also the elegant *a la moda* lock, fashionable in Madrid and Barcelona during the eighteenth century. Miquelet locks of all types continued to be made until well into the nineteenth century.

In all the locks described so far the sears consist of horizontally pivoting levers, of varying degrees of complexity, which secure either the wheel or the cock, depending on the lock type. Probably during the third decade of the seventeenth century, a lock was developed in France – the 'French flintlock' – which combined the L-shaped united frizzen and pan cover with a vertically pivoting sear engaging half- and full-cock notches cut into a tumbler in the manner of a ratchet and pawl – the half-cock notch being undercut so as to prevent accidental disengagement of the sear. A gun of 1630 in the Royal Collection at Windsor Castle (no. L.316; page 32) is the earliest example of a dated flintlock of this type. By around 1670 the French flintlock had achieved a degree of mechanical and aesthetic sophistication, such that its simplicity, reliability and elegance had secured its adoption in most European countries, the Mediterranean lands being, however, largely excepted.

The final quarter of the seventeenth century brought the establishment in France of the influential 'classic Louis XIV style'. This consisted of a flintlock with convex surfaces to the lockplate and cock, combined with an elegant, modern style of stock on long arms, and an equally graceful butt with a spurred cap on pistols – the mounts being of either brass, iron or silver. Pistol butt-caps having slender extensions, or spurs, remained popular until the end of the eighteenth century, and indeed even later in some areas. Around 1700

Double-barrelled flintlock pistol: French, *c.*1670. This is an early example of the Classic Louis XIV Style, applied to an 'over and under' double-barrelled pistol. The right-hand lock fires the upper barrel, the left-hand lock the lower. The locks are signed 'VARNIER A PARIS'. (Pitt-Rivers Museum, Oxford, no. 1938.35.1332)

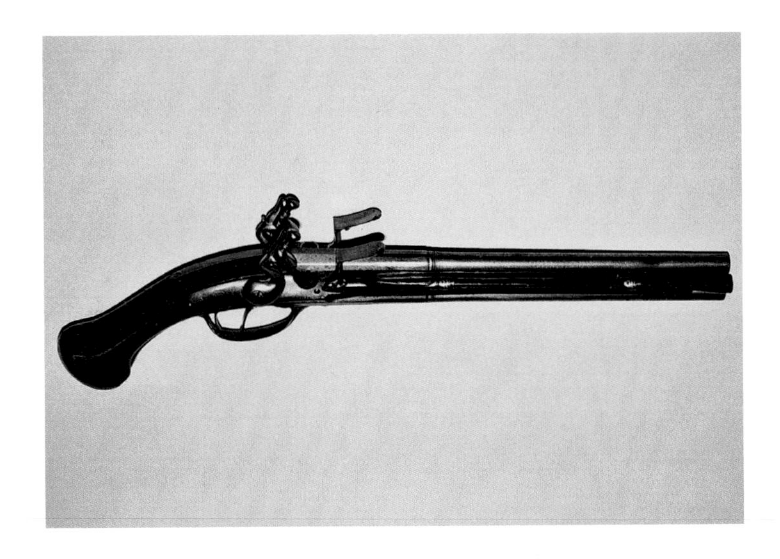

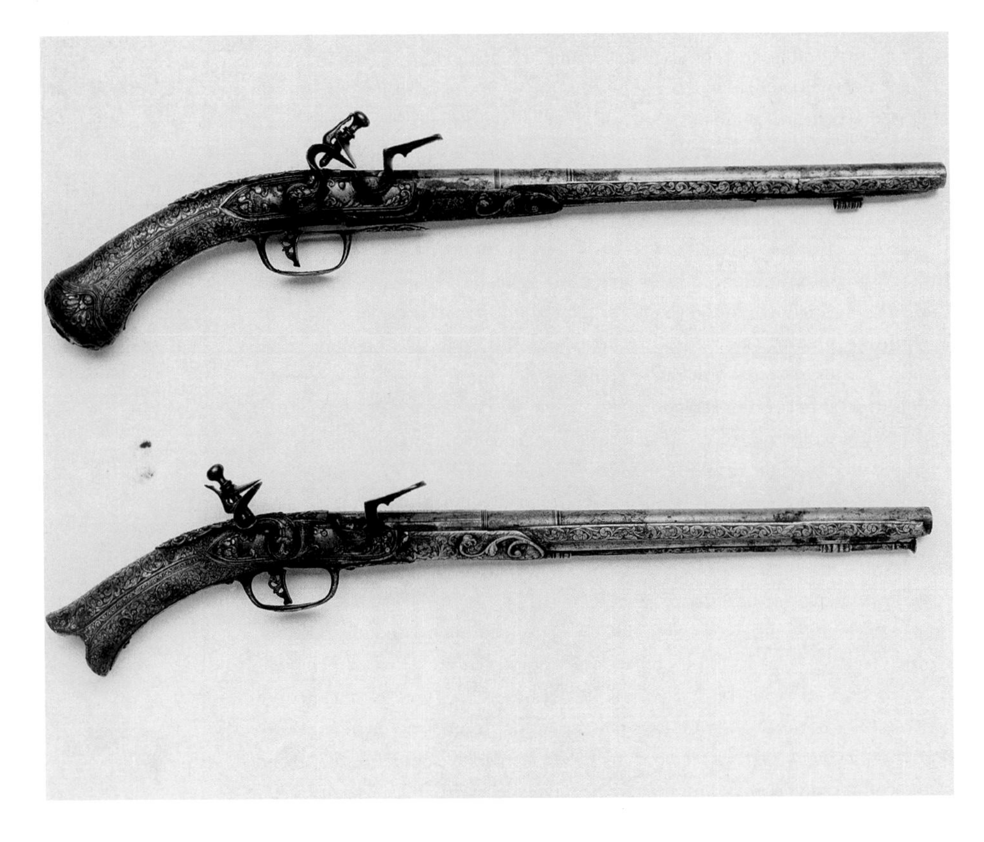

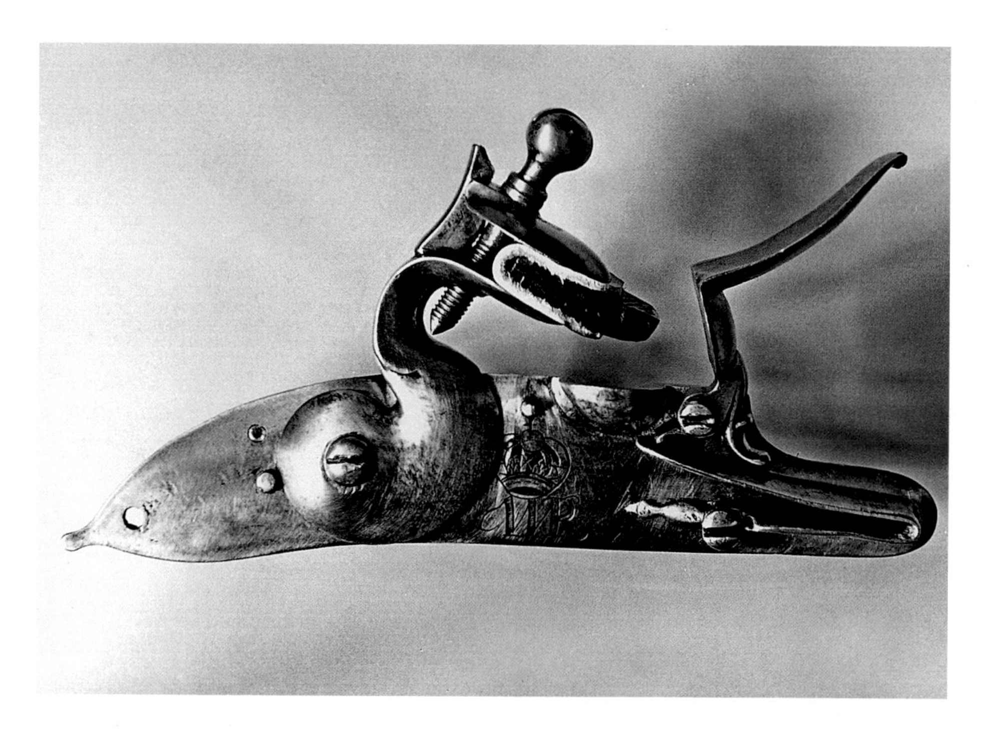

Flintlock: English, c.1695. This lock is from a regulation military musket. It bears the engraved cipher of King William III (1688–1702).

a flat-surfaced lockplate and cock became fashionable in France, although the rounded style remained popular in England for considerably longer.

Another feature of the late seventeenth century was the emergence of military weapons conforming to a specific regulation pattern. This process is first recognisable in England during the reign of King James II (1685–88), and muskets (for infantry) and carbines and pistols (for cavalry) began to have the crowned royal cipher engraved on their lockplates. The previously ubiquitous matchlocks (for muskets) and wheellocks (for pistols and carbines) had, by 1700, virtually disappeared from military use. The superiority of the flintlock, which did away with the need for both a smouldering matchcord and a separate spanner, was by then almost universally recognised.

Opposite:
Pair of 'all-steel' flintlock pistols: Italian, c.1690. All-metal construction is particularly associated with Scottish pistols, but it was also employed elsewhere, as in these examples, whose stocks are of engraved and chiselled iron. The trigger guards are signed 'Hanio Zuccoli in Milano', and the barrels 'LAZARO LAZARINO' for Lazaro Lazarino Cominazzo. Born in 1646, he was a member of a highly distinguished family of barrel-smiths working in Gardone Val Trompia. North Italian barrels of the seventeenth century were highly esteemed for their lightness and strength. (Liverpool Museum, no. M.4778a and b. © National Museums, Liverpool)

THE EIGHTEENTH CENTURY

With regard to the locks, we have nothing material to offer; the genius and industry of the English workmen having already brought them to such a degree of elegance and perfection, that we have scarcely any thing farther to hope for, or require.

John Acton (1789), *An Essay on Shooting.*

THE eighteenth century brought little in the way of fundamental innovation. Aesthetically pleasing design became the norm, with fairly frequent use, for example, of silver mounts, until a more austere mood set in towards the end of the century, especially in England. Technical refinement of the flintlock accompanied these trends. Bridles – metal brackets supporting pivoting parts – had been used on wheellocks during the sixteenth century, and their incorporation into the French type of flintlock mechanism began around 1650. However, a bridle supporting the tumbler became a standard feature on good-quality locks only towards the end of the century; a bridle extending from the flash-pan to support the frizzen screw took longer to become the norm. An anti-friction roller on the toe of the frizzen, or (later) on the frizzen spring itself, became an increasingly common

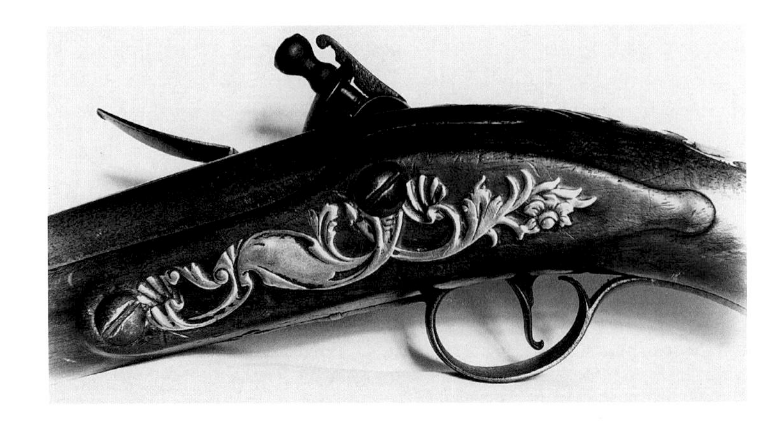

Detail of pistol: English: c.1745. This shows the silver side-plate acting as a decorative washer for the two screws ('side-nails') securing the lock to the stock; two such screws were standard at this time, although three had been common earlier. Also visible are the view and proof marks (V and GP, crowned) of the Worshipful Company of Gunmakers of London, stamped on the barrel at the breech; these guaranteed the safety of the weapon.

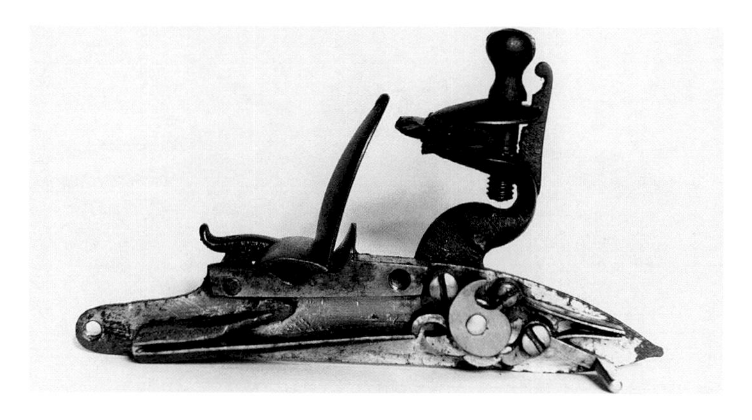

Interior of the lock from the pistol illustrated on page 36. It is signed 'GRIFFIN' for Benjamin Griffin of Bond Street, London. In contrast to the simple lock (of about the same date) illustrated on page 33, this mechanism has a bridle supporting the tumbler axis. The lock is set at half-cock.

feature on English firearms from *c.*1760 onwards, together with a swivel link between the mainspring and the tumbler. These features were slower to find acceptance on the Continent, as was also the introduction of a relatively rain-proof flash-pan. Spanish barrels enjoyed a high reputation throughout

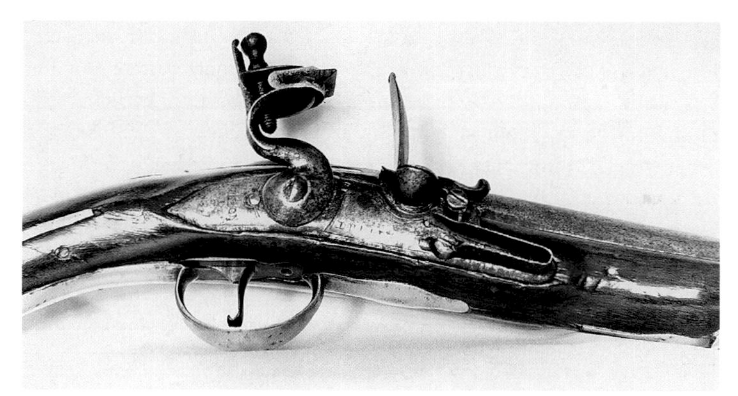

Detail of flintlock pistol: Irish, *c.*1740. This is a long holster pistol of military type by James Wilson of Dublin. The lock is set at full-cock with the pan cover closed; the pistol is ready to fire.

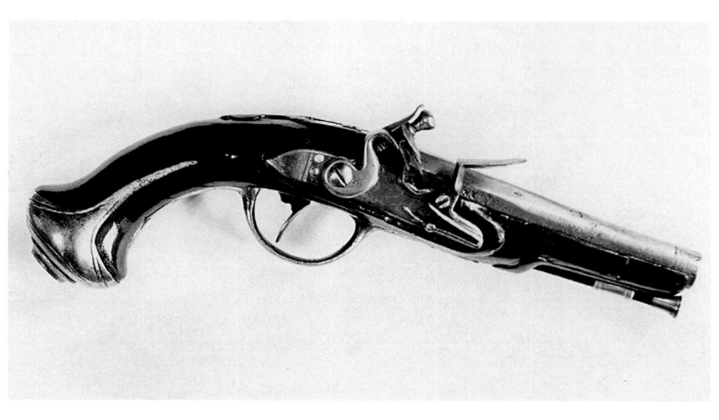

Flintlock pocket pistol: French, *c.*1730. The rounded forms of the Louis XIV style have now given way to a flat lockplate and cock. This is a typical Continental pocket pistol – simply a smaller version of the larger holster pistols carried in pairs at the saddle bow.

Right: Detail of brass-barrelled blunderbuss: English, dated (17)60. Bailey's *Universal Etymological English Dictionary* of 1763 (twentieth edition) defines a blunderbuss as 'a short brass Gun of a large Bore ... carrying small Bullets'. This is misleading; blunderbuss barrels were made of both iron and brass, and the essence of the weapon is that the bore is flared towards the muzzle, giving the (erroneous) impression of spreading the shot. Blunderbusses were popular for home defence, as well as on mail coaches and on board ship.

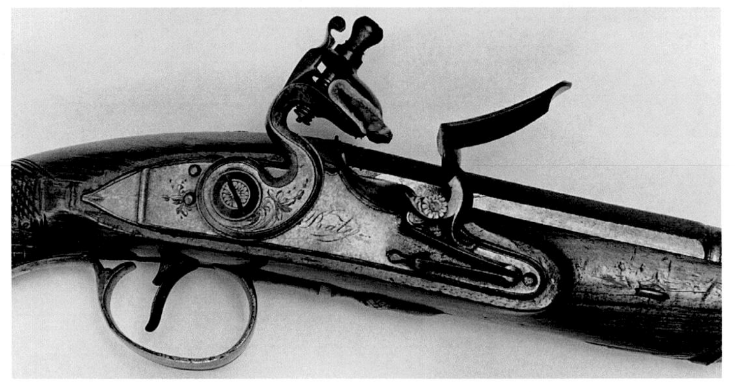

Above: Detail of duelling pistol: English, *c.*1780. Precision pistols (cased in pairs, together with their loading and cleaning accessories) for use in the lethal (and always illegal) practice of duelling first emerged as specialised weapons around 1770, and were initially particularly associated with the London gunmaker Robert Wogdon. They were subsequently manufactured by all the leading gunmakers of the day, such as John Twigg, Durs Egg, Harvey Walklate Mortimer, Henry Nock, and the brothers John and Joseph Manton. This lock has a (by this date standard) bridle from the flash-pan supporting the frizzen screw; there is also an anti-friction roller on the toe of the frizzen where it is in contact with its spring. Both the touch-hole and the flash-pan are gold-lined, and the butt is chequered for a better grip. Edward Bate, the London maker of this pistol, was especially noted for his air-guns.

Right: Interior view of the lock of the pistol illustrated above. The mechanism is set at half-cock. The bridle supporting both the tumbler and the sear screw is visible, as also is the swivel link between the tumbler and the lower arm of the mainspring – another refinement intended to reduce friction.

Wheellock rifle: German (Saxony), dated 1730. This piece illustrates the late survival of the wheellock in parts of the German-speaking world. It was made by Benjamin Reismüller of Bautzen in Saxony. The lock is of the geared variety, and a hair-trigger mechanism is fitted. The butt is of the conventional French pattern – making this a so-called Müllerbüchse ('Miller gun') – rather than the German style more usually encountered on weapons of this type. (Liverpool Museum, no. M.4760. © National Museums, Liverpool)

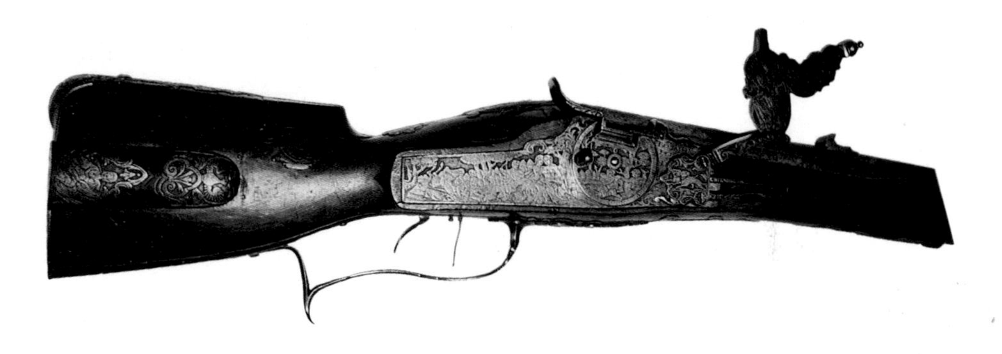

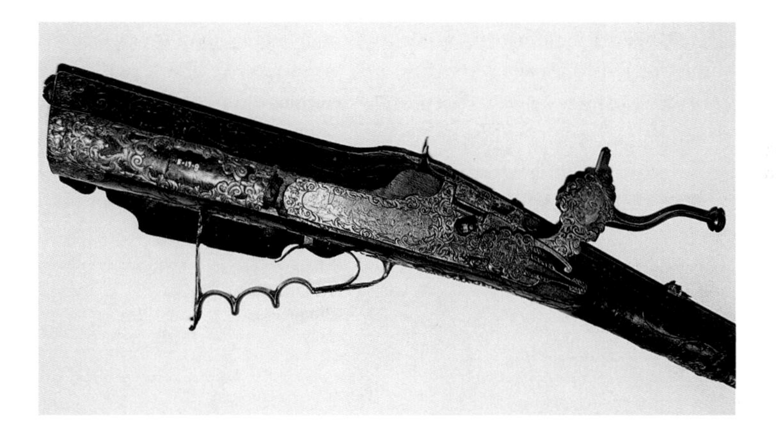

Wheellock rifle: Austrian, *c.*1740. This is another late wheellock rifle, this time with a traditional German cheek-stock. It was made by Franz Xaver Zellner, a member of a distinguished Salzburg gunmaking family. Once again, there is a butt-trap with a sliding cover. (Liverpool Museum, no. 1945.17.8. © National Museums, Liverpool)

the century, and features associated with these, such as a folded or twisted iron construction (for strength), and a gold-lined touch-hole (to reduce corrosion), began to be incorporated into English products, as were also gold-lined flash-pans. By 1800, English pistols and sporting guns exhibited the aesthetics of functionalism, with decorative elements reduced to a minimum. This trend was followed to only a limited extent on the Continent, where elaborate applied ornament remained popular.

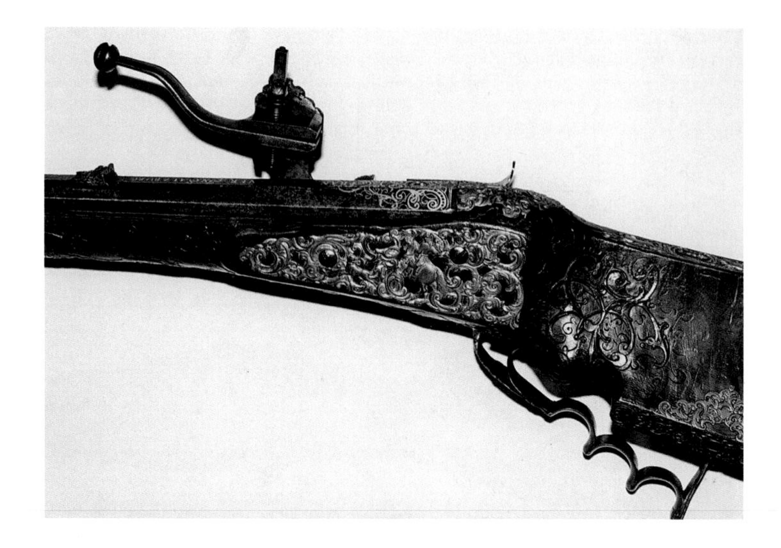

Detail of the left-hand side of the rifle illustrated on page 39 (bottom). (© National Museums, Liverpool)

In contrast to such technical refinements, certain areas continued to produce anachronistic pieces. Central Italy (snaphaunces) and parts of Germany and Austria (wheellocks) have already been mentioned. Pistols of archaic aspect continued to be manufactured in Scotland throughout the eighteenth century, although the elegant fishtail- and lemon-butted weapons of the previous century had ceased to be manufactured after *c.*1650. They were replaced by two new styles, possibly derived from them, the 'scroll' and 'heart' butts, the latter being restricted to eastern Scotland. The stocks on these pistols were usually of iron. A comparable phenomenon was exhibited by the pistols produced in the Catalan town of Ripoll. The wheellock weapons

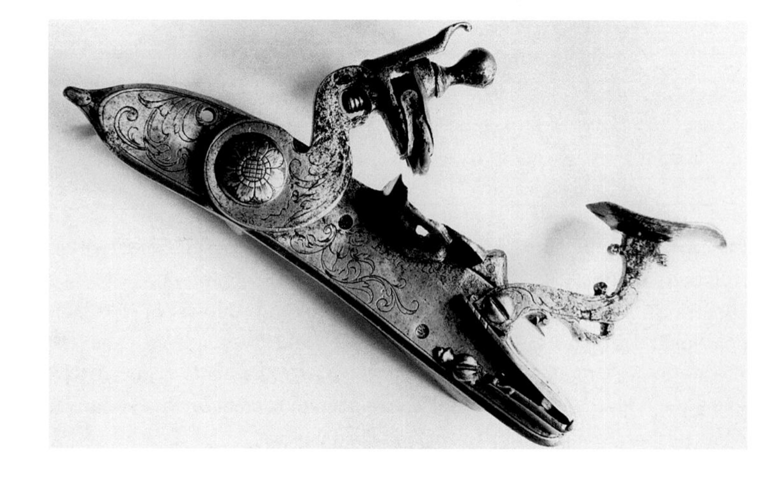

'Florentine' snaphaunce lock: Italian (Marche), *c.*1760. An example of the late survival of the snaphaunce in central Italy. It is signed 'IL BARGIACCHI', a maker who appears to have worked in Pesaro.

Flintlock belt pistol: Scottish, c.1780. This silver-inlaid, iron-stocked pistol has the classic Scottish 'scroll' butt; its maker, John Murdoch of Doune, died in 1812. The lock mechanism is mechanically similar to that on the musket illustrated on page 29 (centre); the principal difference is that the half-cock sear passes through the lockplate to engage the breast of the cock, rather than working on the tumbler. This variety of flintlock, which is typical for such pistols, is sometimes called a 'Highland' lock. A touch-hole pricker with a bulbous head is screwed into the butt between the scrolls.

of the early seventeenth century were replaced after about 1660 by two successive types of miquelet. The typical Ripoll pistol of the eighteenth century was a short, ball-butted weapon of almost sixteenth-century appearance, and manufacture continued into the early nineteenth century.

Refinement of military firearms continued throughout the century. A particularly elegant musket developed in England; known affectionately as 'Brown Bess' (probably from the colour of the stock), it was distinguished by a round-surfaced lock, and a butt having a characteristically high comb together with a prominent 'handrail' wrist. The barrel was designed to accept a socket bayonet, which fitted over the muzzle. It was officially known as the 'Long Land Musket', and the locks and barrels were manufactured by contractors (e.g. Farmer, Galton, Jordan) to the Board of Ordnance, principally in Birmingham, and the complete weapons were then assembled at the Tower of London. The locks typically bear the name of the contractor and their date of manufacture, a process that was discontinued in 1764; thereafter the word 'TOWER' alone appeared. The earliest example in the Royal Armouries at Leeds (no. XII.1687) is dated 1718; early pieces were mounted in iron, but from 1727 (on the basis of lock dates) onwards brass was standard. As at around 1750, Brown Bess and her family may be summarised as follows:

1. Long Land Musket: 46 inch (117 cm) barrel of 0.76 inch (19 mm) calibre, for infantry.
2. Short Land Musket: 42 inch (107 cm) barrel of 0.76 inch (19 mm) calibre, for dragoons (traditionally mounted infantry).
3. Carbine without Bayonet for Horse: 37 inch (94 cm) barrel of 0.66 inch (17 mm) calibre, for cavalry.
4. Land Service Pistol: 12 inch (30 cm) barrel of 0.66 inch (17 mm) or 0.56 inch (14 mm) calibre, for mounted troops (including dragoons), pistols being issued in pairs and carried in saddle holsters.

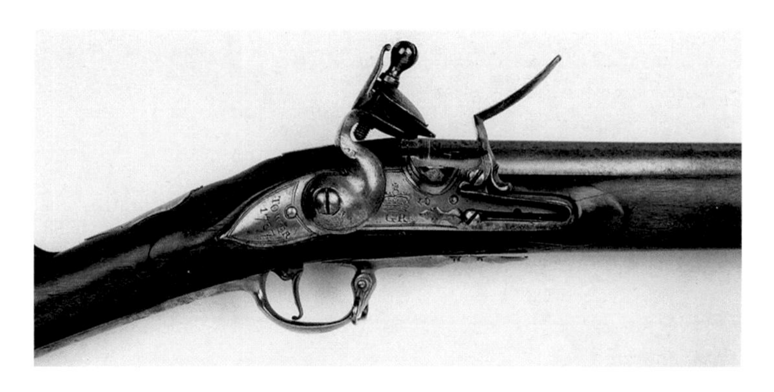

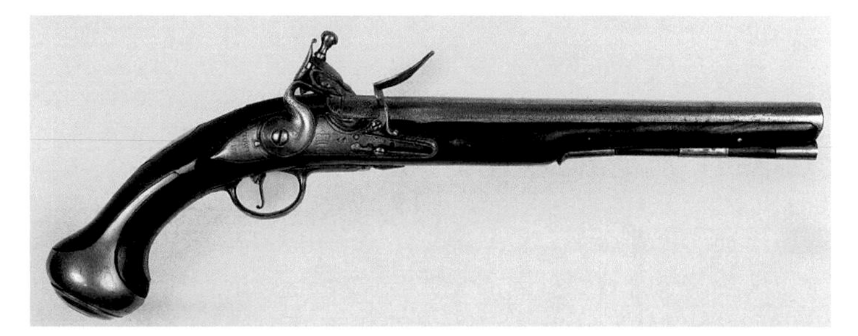

Top:
'Long Land Musket': English, dated 1727. The lock is engraved with the crowned cipher of either King George I (1714–27) or George II (1727–60). It is dated 1727 and engraved 'TOWER', indicating its place of manufacture at the Tower of London. It represents the earliest type of brass-mounted 'Brown Bess' musket. (National Army Museum, no. 1990.02.55.1. Courtesy of the Council of the National Army Museum, London)

Middle:
'Land Service Pistol': English, dated 1725. This weapon is also brass-mounted and marked 'TOWER'. Such weapons were carried in pairs in saddle holsters by both 'horse' and dragoons. (National Army Museum, no. 1975.06.68. Courtesy of the Council of the National Army Museum, London)

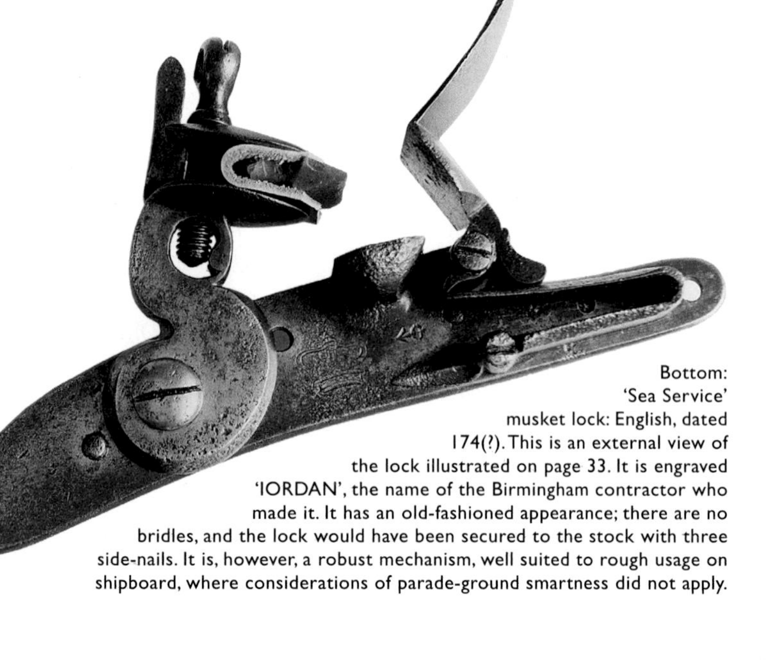

Bottom:
'Sea Service' musket lock: English, dated 174(?). This is an external view of the lock illustrated on page 33. It is engraved 'IORDAN', the name of the Birmingham contractor who made it. It has an old-fashioned appearance; there are no bridles, and the lock would have been secured to the stock with three side-nails. It is, however, a robust mechanism, well suited to rough usage on shipboard, where considerations of parade-ground smartness did not apply.

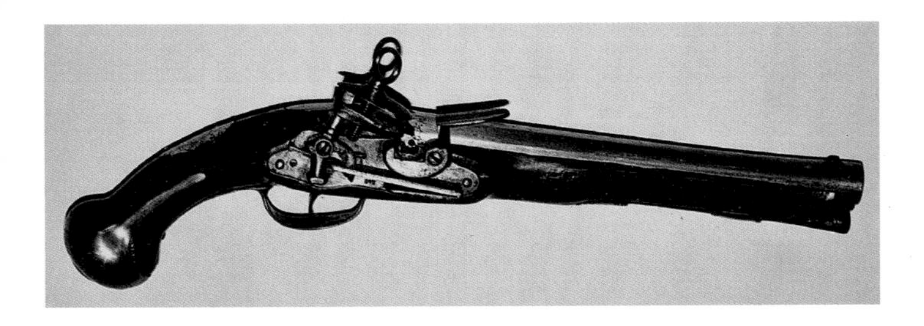

Miquelet lock holster pistol: Spanish, dated 1799. This pistol illustrates the enduring popularity of the *patilla* lock in Spain. It is an example of the Royal Horse Guards model of 1789. The barrel bears the date and the mark of Bartolomé de Arluciaga, a barrel-maker of Elgóibar, a town close to the Basque manufacturing centre of Placencia, where the Royal Arms Factory was located. (Pitt-Rivers Museum, Oxford, no. 1884.27.78)

5. Sea Service Musket: 37 inch (94 cm) barrel of 0.78 inch (20 mm) calibre, for shipboard use.
6. Sea Service Pistol: 12 inch (30 cm) barrel of 0.56 inch (14 mm) calibre, for shipboard use.

Sea service weapons had an old-fashioned appearance, with flat locks and ring-necked cocks. Bayonets for muskets were not an Admiralty requirement until 1752. Following the outbreak of the Seven Years War in 1756, a wider range of weapons was gradually introduced, partly in connection with the establishment of light troops – light dragoons and light infantry.

In France development followed a different course. From 1728, the national armouries of Charleville, St Étienne, Tulle and Maubeuge produced a series of muskets in which the barrel was secured to the stock with three metal barrel bands, rather than the older method of loops on the underside retained by cross-pins. This gave French military firearms, and those copied from them by other nations, a quite different (and perhaps more modern) appearance from that of their English counterparts.

All the weapons described so far (apart from the very earliest) have had detachable locks mounted (usually) on the right-hand side of the stock. Around the middle of the seventeenth century a different arrangement for pistols appeared – possibly first in the Low Countries – in which the breech was forged in one piece with a frame on which the mechanical lock parts

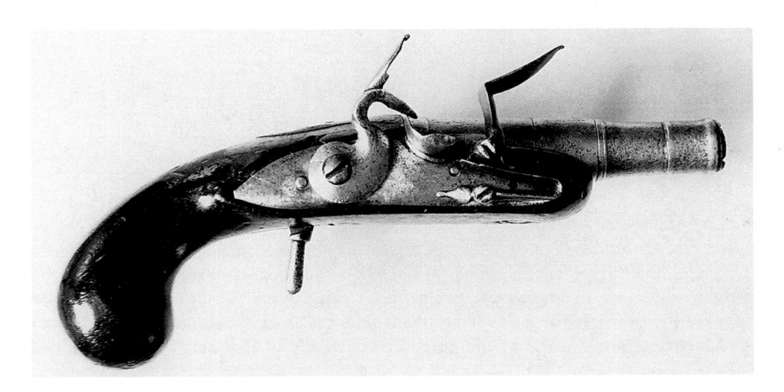

Flintlock pocket pistol: English: c.1700. This is a 'turn-off' pistol with a standard side-lock. The barrel bears the maker's mark of Thomas Hawley, who was Master of the London Gunmakers' Company in 1701. The barrel has decorative turnings imitating those on a cannon.

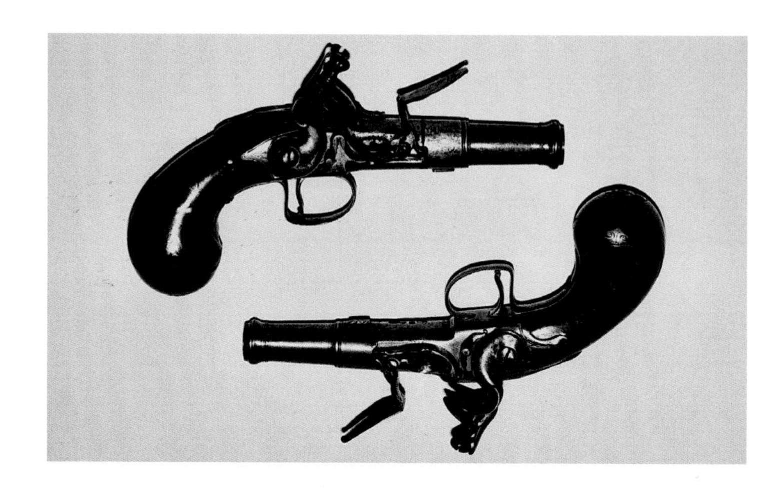

Pair of flintlock pocket pistols: English, *c.*1720. These pistols have box-locks, which retain, however, the conventional positioning of the cock and frizzen on the right-hand side of the weapon. They are also turn-off breech-loaders, and the lug for the barrel wrench can be seen on the underside of each barrel about half-way along from the trigger guard. They were made by William Turvey, who was Master of the London Gunmakers' Company in 1733. Once again, cannon barrels are apparent – a very popular feature on turn-off pistols for most of the eighteenth century. Pistols of this type are sometimes called 'Queen Anne' pistols, although the vast majority date from after her reign (1702–14). (Pitt-Rivers Museum, Oxford, no. 1942.1.364)

were mounted. The stock, hitherto the element which bound together the constituent parts of the piece, was relegated to the role of a grip for the hand. This type of mechanism is known as a 'box lock', and was originally constructed with the cock and frizzen in the traditional place on the right-hand side. However, around 1740 a true box construction emerged in which the cock and frizzen were situated on top of the frame in the mid-line; although also made in France and the Low Countries, this was overwhelmingly an English phenomenon. It was compact, and thus

Flintlock pocket pistol: English, *c.*1745–50. This is a true box-lock pistol, with the cock and frizzen mounted centrally. It is also a turn-off pistol, the trigger guard sliding forward to act as a safety catch by blocking the cock in the half-cock position. It was made by Joseph Clarkson, whose name appears on the right-hand side of the frame, 'LONDON' appearing on the left-hand side. This arrangement is an early feature, as is the single-necked cock and the stepped inletting of the wood of the butt into the frame of the lock. The butt is inlaid with silver wire.

Flintlock pistol: English, 1782–3. This large box-lock pistol is shown with its turn-off barrel unscrewed, ready for loading. It is signed 'BUMFORD'; the maker's name now appears on the left-hand side of the frame, with 'LONDON' on the right. This is a late feature, as is also the ring-necked cock (for strength) and the D-shaped inletting of the butt into the frame. The silver butt-cap bears the Birmingham hallmarks for 1782–83.

particularly well suited to pocket pistols, whose barrels were typically of the 'turn-off' type. This was the commonest breech-loading system of the eighteenth century, having first become popular after about 1660. The barrel was unscrewed, and powder and ball were deposited in the breech. The barrel was then tightened over the soft lead ball with a special wrench. This gave the ball a particularly tight fit, with a powerful pistol as the result. The box-lock arrangement was destined for a long life; it is still the basis of the lockwork in all modern revolvers and automatic pistols.

Flintlocks continued to be made until well into the nineteenth century. The United States Army introduced a new model of flintlock pistol in 1836, and Russian examples are known dated as late as 1852.

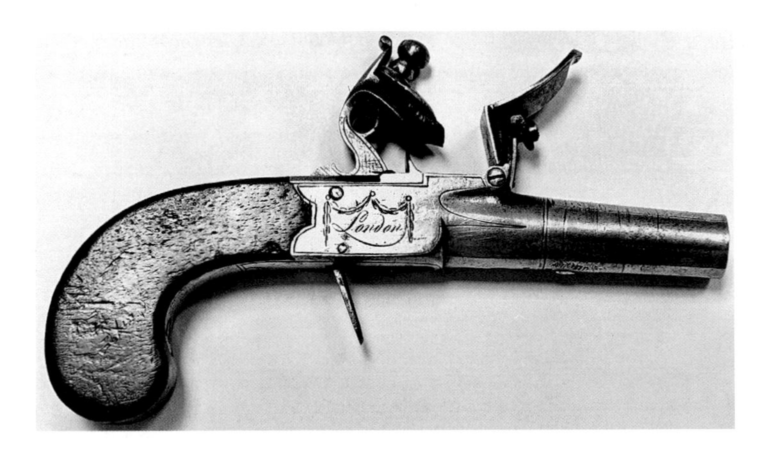

Flintlock pocket pistol: English, c.1795. Although marked 'LONDON', this pistol was made by Thomas Ketland of Birmingham. The cannon barrel has now given way to a simpler design of plain profile, and the frizzen spring is mounted on top of the pan cover, rather than being recessed into the top of the breech. There is no trigger guard; the trigger snaps out of the frame automatically when the pistol is brought to full-cock.

POSTSCRIPT

FULMINATING MERCURY ... detonates loudly ... by the blow of a hammer.

James Parkinson (1809), *The Chemical Pocket Book*.

THE percussion system '*...of Discharging or Giving Fire to Artillery and all other Firearms*', in which a chemical compound (typically fulminate of mercury) is detonated by a hammer blow, was patented (no. 3032) by the Scottish clergyman Alexander Forsyth on 11th April 1807. This ignition system is intrinsically reliable, and it freed firearms design from the restrictions imposed by the earlier sparking locks. Its introduction ushered in a range of increasingly sophisticated weapons, whose rate of development was particularly brisk during the nineteenth century; Samuel Colt's first factory at Paterson, New Jersey, commenced production of revolvers in 1836, and the first bolt-action rifle (its breech mechanism working on the principle of the common door bolt), the Dreyse 'needle gun' (so called from its long firing-pin), was issued to the Prussian army on a limited scale in 1841. Detonating compound contained in a small copper cap proved the most satisfactory arrangement, at first in combination with loose powder and ball, as previously, but, from the 1850s onwards, increasingly united with the propellant and projectile in a self-contained and waterproof copper- or brass-cased cartridge. Smokeless powder (nitrocellulose), which is more powerful than traditional black powder, was first applied in the French Lebel army rifle of 1886. Automatic fire, in which the otherwise troublesome recoil is used as a source of energy to reload and recock the weapon, was successfully realised by the American Hiram Maxim in 1884. The first commercially successful automatic small-arm was the Mauser pistol of 1896, and this essentially modern weapon provides a convenient point at which to end this story.

FURTHER READING

Most books on early firearms are regrettably now out of print and available only from specialist booksellers. What follows is a selection of some of the most important studies.

Bailey, D. W. *British Military Firearms: 1715–1815*. Arms and Armour Press, London, 1971.

Baxter, D. R. *Superimposed Load Firearms*. South China Morning Post, Hong Kong, 1966.

Blackmore, H. L. *British Military Firearms*. Herbert Jenkins, London, 1961.

Blackmore, H. L. *Firearms*. Dutton Vista, London, 1964.

Blackmore, H. L. *Guns and Rifles of the World*. Batsford, London, 1965.

Blackmore, H. L. *Royal Sporting Guns at Windsor*. H.M.S.O., London, 1968.

Blair, C. *Pistols of the World*. Batsford, London, 1968.

Blair, C. (editor) *Pollard's History of Firearms*. Country Life, Feltham, 1983.

Blair, C. *Scottish Firearms*. Museum Restoration Service, Bloomfield, 1995.

Carpegna, N. di *Brescian Firearms*. Edizioni de Luca, Rome, 1997.

Gaibi, A. *Armi da Fuoco Portatili Italiane*. Bramante, Milan, 1968 and 1978.

Hayward, J. F. *European Firearms*. H.M.S.O., London, 1955 and 1969.

Hayward, J. F. *The Art of the Gunmaker. I*. Barrie & Rockliff, London, 1962 and 1965.

Hayward, J. F. *The Art of the Gunmaker. II*. Barrie and Rockliff, London, 1963.

Hoff, A. *Feuerwaffen. I & II*. Klinkhardt u. Biermann, Brunswick, 1969.

Hoff, A. *Dutch Firearms*. Sotheby, Parke Bernet, London, 1978.

Lavin, J. D. *A History of Spanish Firearms*. Herbert Jenkins, London, 1965.

Lenk, T. *The Flintlock: its Origin and Development*. Holland Press, London, 1965.

Neal, W. K. *Spanish Guns and Pistols*. Bell, London, 1955.

Neal, W. K. and Back, D. H. L. *The Mantons: Gunmakers*. Herbert Jenkins, London, 1967.

Needham, J. *Science and Civilization in China. V:7*. C.U.P., Cambridge, 1986.

Partington, J. R. *A History of Greek Fire and Gunpowder*. Heffer, Cambridge, 1960.

Peterson, H. L. (editor) *Encyclopaedia of Firearms*. Connoisseur, London, 1964.

Schedelmann, H. *Die Grossen Büchsenmacher*. Klinkhardt u. Biermann, Brunswick, 1972.

Spencer, M. G. and Philpott, F. A. *Early European Hand-Firearms in Liverpool Museum*. Alan Sutton, Stroud, 1992.

Terenzi, M. *Gli Armaioli Anghiaresi*. Marte, Rome, 1972: reprinted in Diotalleri, D. *Fuochi d'Anghiari*. Petruzzi, Arezzo, 2003.

Also, articles in: *Journal of the Arms and Armour Society*. Leatherhead, 1953.

PLACES TO VISIT

Foremost among museums in the United Kingdom are the following. Not all museums have their collections on public display all the time, so it is usually worth telephoning before a visit.

Kelvingrove Art Gallery and Museum, Argyle Street, Glasgow G3 8AG. Telephone: 0141 276 9599.
Website: www.glasgowmuseums.com

National Museum of Scotland, Chambers Street, Edinburgh EH1 1JF. Telephone: 0131 225 7534.
Website: www.nms.ac.uk

Pitt-Rivers Museum, South Parks Road, Oxford OX1 3PP.
Telephone: 01865 270927. Website: www.prm.ox.ac.uk

Royal Armouries, Armouries Drive, Leeds LS10 1LT.
Telephone: 0113 220 1916.
Website: www.armouries.org.uk

Victoria and Albert Museum, Cromwell Road, London SW7 2RL. Telephone: 0207 942 2000. Website: www.vam.ac.uk

Wallace Collection, Manchester Square, London W1U 3BN.
Telephone: 0207 563 9500.
Website: www.wallacecollection.org

World Museum Liverpool, William Brown Street, Liverpool L3 8EN. Telephone: 0151 478 4393.
Website: www.liverpoolmuseums.org.uk

Europe is dominated by the great dynastic armouries at Vienna (Kunsthistorisches Museum), Madrid (Real Armería) and Dresden (Historisches Museum). The Musée de l'Armée in Paris (Hôtel des Invalides) has holdings of the greatest importance, as does also the much smaller Armoury of the Council of Ten in Venice (Palazzo Ducale). The Landeszeughaus in Graz, Austria, is a unique survival of a provincial arsenal of the sixteenth and seventeenth centuries. The collections in Stockholm (Livrustkammaren) and Copenhagen (Tøjhusmuseet) are outstanding, as are those in St. Petersburg (Hermitage) and Moscow (Kremlin). The finest collection in the United States is that in the Metropolitan Museum of Art, New York.

INDEX

Arquebus 4
Blunderbuss 38
Breech-loaders
  "Snuff box" 18, 19, 21, 22
  "Turn off" 43, 44, 45
Brown Bess 41, 42
Carbine 16, 35, 41
Flintlock
  Early 26
  "English" 28, 29
  "French" 32, 33
  Late 45
  Principle 24
  Mediterranean – see Miquelet
Gunpowder
  Composition 4
  Invention 4
  Smokeless 46
Hand-gun
  Chinese 4, 5
  Earliest 4, 5
  European 6, 7, 8, 9
Magazine arms 23
Matchlock
  Chinese 8
  Early 5, 6
  European 6, 7, 8, 9
  Late 8, 9
  Military 6, 7, 8, 9
  Principle 6
Miquelet
  Italian 30, 32
  Portuguese 30, 33
  Spanish 30, 31, 43
Musket
  British 6, 28, 29, 35, 41, 42
  Definition 6
  French 43
Percussion lock
  Invention 46
  Principle 46
Pistol
  Box-lock 43, 44, 45
  Duelling 38
  Early 10, 11, 16
  Military 22, 41, 42, 43
  Pocket 26, 27, 29, 37, 43, 44, 45
  Ripoll 16, 40, 41
  Scottish 28, 30, 40, 41
Revolver
  Colt 46
  Early 10, 22
Rifle
  Early 19
  Principle 19
Sights 5, 19
Snaphaunce
  Early 24, 26
  English 25, 26, 27
  Italian 30, 31, 40
  Principle 26
  Scandinavian 26, 27
  Scottish 27, 28, 29
Wheellock
  Early 9, 11, 12, 14
  English 17, 22
  French 14, 15, 17
  Geared 20, 39
  German 14, 16, 18, 19, 20
  Italian 13, 15, 16
  Late 23, 39, 40
  Principle 9, 11
  Self-spanning 18, 22